Praise for *Lean Body, Fat Wallet*

Finally a book that deals with two of the main issues women are concerned with—what we see in the mirror and what we see in our bank accounts! *Lean Body, Fat Wallet* provides practical tips to improve your health and your finances. But Danna and Ellie go deeper than that; they address the core issues that most impact those areas—our habits. They share four habits from their own lives to create a new way of thinking that will become second nature. What a gift to have two personal coaches take us step-by-step to a whole new way to live.

—SHEILA WALSH, AUTHOR
OF *THE STORM INSIDE*

In *Lean Body, Fat Wallet* Ellie and Danna connect the unique path to physical and financial health. I love their straightforward approach that centers on practical change every reader can make happen for themselves. This book proves the power of positive thinking and positive action—no matter how small—can lead to amazing, life-altering change. A must read!

—JILL SAVAGE, CEO OF HEARTS AT
HOME AND AUTHOR OF *LIVING WITH
LESS SO YOUR FAMILY HAS MORE*

Lean Body, Fat Wallet is packed with powerful advice to give every woman two of her most desired goals—more money and fewer pounds! Written in an easy-to-understand, easy-to-apply style, it is like having your two best friends give you wise insights over a warm latte—it is comforting, yet energizes you for action! I know Ellie and Danna, and they live out each word and are amazing role models and coaches helping women worldwide live the lives they dream of.

—PAM FARREL, INTERNATIONAL SPEAKER, AUTHOR
OF OVER 38 BOOKS, INCLUDING BEST-SELLING *MEN
ARE LIKE WAFFLES, WOMEN ARE LIKE SPAGHETTI*
AND *THE 10 BEST DECISIONS A WOMAN CAN MAKE*

Ellie and Danna "make the connection" in this transformational book that is sure to get men and woman on the right track to physical and financial fitness. The documented truths they reveal are informative, entertaining, and challenging. This is a guide that will be constantly referred to and recommended!

—DEBORAH SMITH PEGUES, BEST-SELLING
AUTHOR OF 30 DAYS TO TAMING YOUR TONGUES

In today's distracted world, two of the most difficult challenges in life are achieving a lean body and fat wallet. But Danna and Ellie have figured out the secrets, and we can't read fast enough. The challenges of work, travel, and stress in the entertainment industry make this required reading, and we both highly recommend it.

—KATHLEEN AND PHIL COOKE, FILMMAKERS,
MEDIA CONSULTANTS, AND FOUNDERS OF COOKE
PICTURES, IN LOS ANGELES, CALIFORNIA

Lean Body
Fat Wallet

discover the
powerful connection
to help you
lose weight,
dump debt, and
save money

Ellie Kay & Danna Demetre

NELSON
BOOKS

An Imprint of Thomas Nelson

Published in Nashville, Tennessee, by Nelson Books, an imprint of Thomas Nelson. Nelson Books and Thomas Nelson are registered trademarks of HarperCollins Christian Publishing, Inc.

Authors are represented by the Steve Laube Agency, LLC, 5025 N. Central Avenue, #635, Phoenix, Arizona 85012.

Thomas Nelson, Inc., titles may be purchased in bulk for educational, business, fundraising, or sales promotional use. For information, please e-mail SpecialMarkets@ ThomasNelson.com.

Names and identifying details of some people mentioned in this book have been changed to protect their privacy.

The websites and organizations recommended in this book are intended as resources for the reader. These websites are not intended in any way to be or to imply an endorsement on behalf of Thomas Nelson, nor does the publisher vouch for online content for the life of this book.

This book is not intended to provide therapy, counseling, clinical advice, or treatment or to take the place of clinical advice and treatment from your personal physician or professional mental health counselor. Readers are advised to consult their own qualified health-care physicians regarding mental health or medical issues. Neither the publisher nor the author takes any responsibility for any possible consequences from any treatment, action, or application of information in this book to the reader.

Scripture quotations are taken from the NEW AMERICAN STANDARD BIBLE®, © The Lockman Foundation 1960, 1962, 1963, 1968, 1971, 1972, 1973, 1975, 1977, 1995. Used by permission.

Library of Congress Cataloging-in-Publication Data

Kay, Ellie.
   Lean body, fat wallet : discover the powerful connection to help you lose weight, dump debt, and save money / Ellie Kay and Danna Demetre.
      pages cm
   Includes bibliographical references.
   ISBN 978-1-4002-0553-0
1. Habit breaking—Religious aspects—Christianity. 2. Food—Religious aspects—Christianity. 3. Food habits. 4. Finance, Personal—Religious aspects—Christianity. 5. Debt. 6. Saving and investment. I. Title.
   BV4598.7.K39 2013
   248.4—dc23

                              2013019749

From Ellie

To the kids I chased in order to have a lean body: Daniel, Philip, Bethany, Jonathan, and Joshua, as well as Jenn and Melissa, my daughters in love. And to my husband, Bob, who worked with me to acquire a fat wallet and has been my life partner for more than a quarter of a century: I could not have done this without your love and support. My greatest joy is to see all of you walk in truth.

From Danna

To my beautiful adult daughters, Jamie and Jill: I know you have struggled (as I did) with habits of body and bank. I am thankful and proud that you live many of the healthy habits we teach in this book. It is so much fun to practice them with you and enjoy our deep friendship.

To the love of my life, Lew: it is a joy to be married to a man to whom healthy living comes naturally. You keep me motivated to live an intentional life that makes meaningful deposits to those God has placed in our path. I adore doing life with you!

Contents

Introduction

The Power of Physical and Fiscal Synergy

Imagine making simple lifestyle changes that can help you get leaner, healthier, debt-free, and wealthier . . . all at the same time. Losing debt and excess fat simultaneously seems too good to be true—but you can! As life experts in two seemingly different fields, we have discovered that the principles and habits that are good for your wallet are equally good for your body.

Most people lead overly busy and stressful lives. We get stuck in bad habits and assume the changes needed are so difficult that we might as well give up before even starting. That misconception keeps many of us stuck. However, when we practice consistently a few simple habits, we can transform our lives in amazing ways. When we stop making excuses and replace that negative energy with positive action, the results can be amazing.

In *Lean Body, Fat Wallet*, we will teach you four simple habits that you can practice in the physical and fiscal areas of your life. Once you learn and implement them in one area, you will have a foundation to build upon in the other area as well. Whether you are dealing with the temptation to overeat or overspend, or desiring to change your core thoughts about food and money, these four strategies can serve you well for life. These core habits will eventually become your autopilot response so that you are no longer relying on self-discipline and willpower alone to reach your health and wealth goals.

Recently, my (Danna's) daughter Jill lost some weight and improved her overall fitness. As she reviewed the chapters of this book, she remembered that she had read the introduction to a few of the habits about a year ago. She was surprised and delighted to discover that her implementation of these strategies had made the biggest difference in her recent transformation. She was amazed that such simple changes produced significant and lasting results!

How different would your life be if you were out of debt? What would you do if you lost all your excess weight or had energy to burn? Who would you help, where would you invest, how would you sleep at night if you had more money in the bank than you've ever had?

The simple and practical strategies in this book will inspire you to explore these questions with hope and expectation. You can accomplish lasting change in your health and finances by practicing these principles and adopting these habits.

We wish you great success as you make small steps toward lasting change in your body and much more than change in your fat wallet!

PART 1

Discover the Four Lean Body, Fat Wallet Habits

Habits for Health and Wealth

Discover a new way to approach your
financial and physical challenges!

The twenty-year-old nursing student fumbled for the key to her apartment as she juggled several heavy textbooks and a grocery sack stuffed with her recent purchases from the local minimart. Once in the door, she dropped the books on the kitchen table, kicked off her shoes, and rummaged through the sack until she found the bag of cookies she was looking for. She knew her roommate would not be home for at least two hours, so she flopped down on the couch, turned on the television, and began to decompress from her long day of classes. With a glass of milk and the bag of cookies in front of her on the coffee table, she surrendered to the inevitable battle she lost every day at this time—the battle of food calling her name and compelling her to binge.

One cookie led to two, then three. She knew she couldn't stop, so she didn't. Since she was sure of the final outcome, she gave in to eating every cookie in the bag. Then she purged to destroy the evidence before her roommate got home. She felt guilty about her overeating. Some days she binged and purged four or five times. The only reason she was not morbidly obese was because she was a master of eating only when she had the freedom to purge immediately. She was also skilled at camouflaging the excess twenty-five pounds she wore as a constant reminder of her ugly secret.

That young woman was me, Danna. For sixteen years, I struggled with emotional eating and, for many of those years, with bouts of bulimia. It seemed the only way I could gain control was to take diet pills. When the shame of my eating disorder became unbearable or I gained weight despite the purging, I'd take amphetamines for weeks or even months and barely eat at all. In the privacy of my mind, I believed the lie that I could not stop overeating. The lie led me down a path of self-loathing that could have completely destroyed my health. As a result of my unhealthy thinking and lifestyle, I also struggled with unrelenting panic attacks for almost five years. Fear perpetuated fear, and I began to believe I was losing my mind. Some days my symptoms were so severe I actually believed I was dying.

At the time, I did not realize I was telling myself lies. I certainly had no understanding that these lies were the root of many of my problems. My constant focus on the misconception that I could not control my unhealthy eating or take charge over my anxiety created damaging thought patterns that dug deeper and more destructive mental ruts in my mind. I constantly told myself, *I can't stop bingeing. I'll never change. I can't lose weight. I'm losing my mind. I might be dying.* The result was a spiral of increasingly harmful emotions and behavior.

In order to get through nursing classes, I took heavy doses of Valium to minimize my accelerating fear of being out in public. I aced my psych nursing semester as I desperately tried to diagnose my precarious mental state. Poring over the pages of my psychology textbook, I read each description of various mental disorders to see if they described my problems. *Schizophrenic? No, I don't think so. Bipolar? Yeah, maybe—when I'm taking amphetamines. Psychotic? Maybe. Neurotic? Absolutely!*

In this dark and troubling valley of life, I began to seek truth. Through the loving guidance of some wise people, I discovered the power of renewing my mind in a life-changing way. By replacing the lies I believed with truth over and over and over again, I began to notice that the panic attacks came less frequently. And when they did come, they were much less severe. Within one year, they were completely gone. No medicine. No therapy. Just truth overriding lies. Over time, I gained victory over my eating issues as well. I've maintained a lean, healthy body for more than thirty years. But I will never forget how it felt to be in bondage to unhealthy thinking.

The principles Ellie and I share in this chapter are the ones both of us have used to change our habits from the inside out. While your challenges may not be as dramatic as ours, the strategies to discover lasting success over the habits of your mind are the same. Whether you are overeating, overspending, or simply lacking the good habits necessary to effect positive change, this chapter and the ones that follow will empower you to take action that can change your life!

Ellie's Story

When I searched for my knight in shining armor, I never expected him to ride in on a jet. My knight turned out to be a pilot named Bob Kay. Time also flew around this guy. When we were dating, we'd linger over pie and coffee at our favorite restaurant. We'd get so caught up in conversation that we were often shocked to discover we'd been talking for hours. I should have clued in to the fact that time was flying when a new shift of waitresses appeared to refill our coffee cups.

When we met, I was an insurance broker making a good salary. I saved, invested, and spent money wisely. Maybe it was my confidence about finances—or maybe just true love—that caused me to overlook Bob's occasional references to "loads of debt" from his prior marriage. He was a man of solid character, which mattered a lot more to me than his finances. Plus, I was marrying into an added bonus of two beautiful stepdaughters as part of the three-for-one deal. Besides, he was a full-time engineer and a part-time pilot, making a good-enough salary, or so I thought.

Bob had graduated from the Air Force Academy and dreamed of one day flying fighter jets. He had flown full time in the active-duty air force but chose to get out of the military after his divorce to be near his daughters. Now he was living the dream, but only part time, as he flew for the National Guard. As we pursued marriage, I told Bob he should pursue his dream of flying jets. Soon after our wedding, Bob went back into the military full time and we were living in active-duty military housing on a captain's salary, which was 15 percent lower than Bob's previous income as an engineer.

Then the credit card bills began to roll in, one by one.

I fully understood what Bob meant by "loads of debt." I'd inherited the financial aftermath of his divorce, which included forty thousand dollars of consumer debt and no assets. In those early years, we had trouble making ends meet and even struggled with the ability to buy groceries. In an attempt at humor, I hung a plaque on the wall that said, "Blessed are the poor, for they be us."

Here is what our portfolio of bills looked like:

- One-third of Bob's income went to income taxes.
- One-third went to child support and medical insurance for Bob's daughters.
- We gave 10 percent of our income to our church and charities.
- We lived on the remaining 23 percent and also serviced our forty thousand dollars of debt.

The situation became even more complicated when Bob and I began to have more babies—a total of five children of our own in seven years. As a blended family, we now had seven children to support. Bob's military career included eleven moves in the first thirteen years of our marriage. It became clear that it would be impractical for me to go back to being a broker, so I stayed home. Besides, I really wanted to be with my children full time.

I also realized that Bob and I had diametrically opposed financial philosophies. He enjoyed living well in his previous life (with the use of credit) and was accustomed to that kind of lifestyle. He considered consumer debt par for the course of any American family. I preferred to live below our means and only buy what we could afford.

He loved to eat out. I winced at every restaurant check. He enjoyed spending money, and I enjoyed saving money. Appraising our dining set (still perfectly good, though I'd bought it at a discount store) one day, he announced he'd like to replace it with something from Ethan Allen.

"We can't afford that!" I exclaimed.

One day I wrote a check for car insurance and a few other bills, and I realized we were down to pennies in our checking account. Bob's next payday wasn't for another week. *This is scary,* I thought. We had some cereal in the pantry and some canned food, but no milk, fruit, or vegetables. Our credit cards were charged to the max. Bob came home in time for us to make the 160-mile round-trip drive from the air force base to suburban Los Angeles to pick up his girls at their grandmother's house. I told him the checkbook news. It was a tense drive to LA.

Arriving at his former mother-in-law's, we found her remodeling her kitchen. The refrigerator was unplugged, and she'd crowded the counter with fruit, vegetables, and canned goods. "You guys wouldn't happen to want any of these, would you?" she asked. "I'm not going to get this fridge going anytime soon." I don't think she knew about our predicament, but there she was, providing for our needs. Bob, wearing his best game face, bagged everything and loaded it into the car. *Charity,* I thought, fighting my emotions. We said nothing on the way home in front of the girls. That night, however, before we went to sleep, it was all I could do to keep from bursting into tears.

"I'm so sorry," Bob whispered, sensing my emotions. "I just couldn't bring myself to admit how the financial baggage from my old life would affect our new family."

He seemed to think that because he had so much debt, he would always be in debt. In fact, a lawyer advised Bob to file for bankruptcy, but he refused. We needed to shift our mind-set from "We will always be in debt" to "We can become debt-free if we develop a plan." We needed to let go of the belief that we had to spend money to have fun. Instead, we began to say, "Fun doesn't have to be centered on spending. We can create our own entertainment without going further into debt."

I suggested that we develop a new strategy for our finances. We agreed on a plan for financial recovery. We would rein in spending, donate 10 percent of our earnings, set aside enough for taxes and child support, and with the roughly 20 percent of Bob's income left over, pay debt and bills.

At first, Bob looked stricken as he contemplated this meager existence, but he wanted to make the kind of changes that would free us from debt. I drew inspiration from my great-grandmother, who'd survived the Great Depression with a simple motto popular at that time: "Use it up, wear it out, make do, do without."

By implementing money-smart strategies, we began to recover. Before long, our cupboards were filled to overflowing, and I had so many groceries that I was able to give them away to food pantries and homeless shelters. We stuck to our budget, never letting down our guard even as the last of Bob's old credit cards were paid off. Two and one half years later, we were completely debt-free and have remained free of consumer debt ever since.

How Do You Change a Habit?

You've heard the saying "How do you eat an elephant? One bite at a time!" That's a good motto for making lasting changes in your habits as well—not by taking one bite at a time, but taking one step at a time. We both faced disastrous lifestyle consequences that were the result of long-standing bad habits. If we had simply looked at the mountain of goals looming before us, we could have easily become discouraged. Instead, we slowly began to take small daily steps toward healthier habits. The strategies in this book are simple, yet they take consistent practice to make a lasting impact.

Learning to implement healthy, lasting habits and *still enjoy life* is the core objective of this book. What's the point of gaining a healthy body and financial security if you are miserable? We believe that the tools we have used for many years will help you design a personalized lifestyle that works best for you.

The Four Lean Body, Fat Wallet Habits

Our lives are driven by a variety of good and bad habits that influence our emotions and behaviors as if we are running on automatic pilot. *Webster's Dictionary* defines *habit* as "an acquired mode of behavior that has become nearly or completely involuntary."[1]

> A habit is something you can do without thinking—which is why most of us have so many of them.
>
> —Frank A. Clark

Our good habits allow us to reap positive rewards, and our bad habits can produce the negative consequences of excessive debt and overweight bodies. When you scan the endless number of books written about these subjects and research the sad statistics related to finding permanent solutions, it becomes obvious that people are still looking for answers. It's not for lack of trying that individuals fail. But *trying* is not enough. We must *train* our minds to respond differently to the challenges we face day after day.

Since our habits have such power in our lives, it makes sense that discovering our bad habits and replacing them with productive ones would be a wise use of our time and energy. With that in mind, we have identified four Lean Body, Fat Wallet Habits that can dramatically transform your body and wallet when implemented consistently.

1. The You Are What You Think Habit
2. The 3D Habit
3. The In and Out Habit
4. The Sustainable Lifestyle Habit

In part one, we will define each so you can understand their significance in your life. We will also discuss each one in a health-and-wealth context. Danna will share how you can add them into your life in simple and effective ways to guide you toward a leaner and healthier body. Ellie will define the four habits from a financial viewpoint and explore ways you can develop a realistic financial strategy for success. In part two, we will discuss these four habits as they apply in various situations to help you build them into all the areas of physical and fiscal wellness.

Before we delve into the first habit in the next chapter, let's explore the top ten reasons we believe people fail to meet their health and wealth goals. We call them "failure factors." It is important to understand what you've been doing wrong so you can make strategic corrections that will move you in a positive direction in the future.

Top Ten Failure Factors

1. You set unrealistic goals.
2. You are driven by the wrong motives.
3. You believe failure is inevitable.
4. You fulfill the need for immediate gratification too often.
5. You are influenced unduly by other people.
6. You practice an all-or-nothing mentality.
7. You rationalize and make excuses rather than taking responsibility.
8. You displace emotional issues through overspending and overeating.

9. You procrastinate rather than taking action.
10. You lack the tools to make compounding incremental change.

Reread the list above and circle any of the failure factors you believe may be significant influences in your life. Later, we will address these factors more specifically in relation to the new habits we are encouraging you to build. We'll show you how you can counteract these success robbers in your life. Failure needs to be seen as a profound learning opportunity.

It's time to stop *trying* so hard and start *training* yourself toward a new way of addressing your health and wealth challenges. Past failures do not need to be repeated. In this book, we will be your coaches to encourage and mentor you toward attainable and sustainable goals.

If Gail Can Change . . . So Can You!

Gail Hayes is a beautiful, vibrant, energetic, and enthusiastic executive leader, life coach, speaker, and educator. In her free time she is a publisher and product development expert. She has been called "an igniter of purpose" because of her passion for life.[2] But a few years ago, Gail was hiding some unhealthy habits that were slowly destroying her physical and financial life. She feared that if others knew, it would discredit her professionally.

In a nutshell, Gail was abusing her body in various ways. Over time, she had become dependent upon large amounts of caffeine to battle lethargy. She did not eat or exercise sufficiently and had increasing aches and pains that further diminished her activity. She counteracted the high of caffeine and other ailments by popping Benadryl (antihistamine) tablets like candy. At first, this over-the-counter medication helped her relax and sleep, but in the long run she found herself in a vicious downward spiral where her body felt constantly itchy and toxic. Additionally, she gorged on sugary, fattening foods and had no idea until she stepped on the scale that she was carrying sixty-five extra pounds on her petite frame. This fact depressed her even more, and some days she didn't have enough energy to get out of bed to walk—which was not practical for a busy, working mother of two active children.

Sadly, Gail's destructive habits were not just limited to her physical health. Her work was suffering, and their family finances were in shambles. Bank accounts were overdrawn, lines of credit were closed, revolving credit cards were denied, and savings were nonexistent. Her finances got so bad that Gail swore her couch had a better credit score than she did. Debt had crept up slowly but surely like a predator and ultimately resulted in Gail's family losing their house to foreclosure.

Fortunately, Gail is a woman of strong faith, and she sensed God telling her that she could be free from her unhealthy habits. She read a Bible verse that said, "Where the Spirit of the Lord is, there is liberty" (2 Cor. 3:17), and she felt the strength to apply wise principles to her health and wealth. With small steps, she formed new habits and broke old patterns. In six short months, Gail shrunk from size 20W to misses' size 12. She looked and felt like a new woman.

There are so many reasons we fall into habits that diminish the quality of our lives. In an effort to avoid uncomfortable circumstances, we rationalize behaviors that actually bring us more pain. Gail can now share openly that her abusive marriage created incredible stress in her life. She felt trapped, alone, and unable to cope. The result was fiscal and physical ruin.

Choose Small Steps toward a New Future

When Gail started to take simple strides toward healthier habits, the pounds began to melt away along with the lethargy and pain. Today she has boundless energy despite being well into her fifties. She recently shared, "I found that when I got my physical life in order, it was much easier to apply similar habits to get my financial life in order as well."

She also broke free from the abuse she had lived with for over two decades.

Gail said, "I realized that you are what you think. Before, I felt like a total failure. Today I feel like a success story." She began to renew her mind with new messages that in turn changed her compulsions and behavior. She also found support in a group of women with whom she can be painfully honest. Before her transformation, a publisher asked her to write books about leadership, but she felt she was a hypocrite and unworthy of the job offer. Fortunately, she learned to tell herself that she *was* worthy and capable, and today she is writing those books. She also continues to implement the daily habits that lead to balance in her physical and financial dimensions of life.

Danna changed her unhealthy eating habits by implementing a new approach to her physical challenges. Ellie turned around her financial difficulties in order to discover habits that led to a vibrant and sustainable approach to money matters. Likewise, Gail was able to make radical changes to her health and wealth by following the habits we describe in this book.

You, too, can discover a new way to approach your financial and physical challenges as you join us in this amazing journey. At the end of this road, you'll discover your very own lean body and fat wallet!

2.

The You Are What
You Think Habit

*Change your habits by changing your thinking
and consistently focusing on new messages.*

"I'm sorry, what's your name again?" Jane asked with a hint of embarrassment in her voice. "I'm just awful at remembering names. Always have been, always will be, I guess!" Seemingly innocent statements like these have much more power than most people imagine.

If you tell yourself the same message over and over, your mind becomes programmed to believe it. Over time, your emotions and actions fall into sync with those words. All of our emotions and actions are driven by our thoughts. If your deeply programmed thoughts are sending you down an unwanted path, it's time to rewire your thinking!

A person is limited only by the thoughts that he chooses.
—James Allen

The Mind—Master of Our Habits

Just as the heart, liver, and kidneys are intended to perform certain vital functions for the body, your brain has been physiologically created to perform crucial functions that impact not only the entire body but also all thoughts, emotions, and actions. The mind—which is the intellectual, thinking, processing aspect of the brain—is essentially in charge. Your life is driven by your interpretation of sights, sounds, tastes, smells, and feelings. The outflow of those interpretations becomes your thoughts, words, and actions. Since your fleshy computer has so much power, it's helpful to understand how this magnificent glob is designed and see why it does what it does! We can better appreciate the complexity of our feelings and behaviors when we understand the physiology of the human brain.

Like a computer, your brain does not place judgment on the data it stores. True or false, it just categorizes the input day after day. But all the data stored is not equal. In your mind, the most dominant thoughts win. In other words, the things you hear, see, think, and say *most often* drive your emotions and behaviors most profoundly. And that is how good and bad habits are formed. You simply respond with consistency to a variety of input based on frequency and intensity.

As brain science researcher Dr. Caroline Leaf, PhD, states in her book *Who Switched Off My Brain?*, "What you think about expands and grows, taking on a life of its own. The direction life takes could be positive or negative; you get to choose. What you choose to think about can foster joy, peace and happiness or the complete opposite."[1]

This reality is profound: if you can change your thoughts, you can change your habits. Rather than trying to get lean and healthy by pure discipline or trying to get your finances in order by using focused willpower, wouldn't it be liberating to do these things as naturally as if you were running on automatic pilot? It's possible—even probable—if you do the proper training.

Dr. Leaf continues by saying, "Remember, our behavior follows our thoughts, not the other way around. Analyzing and addressing our thoughts are key components of conquering habits and behaviors that seem to hold us hostage."[2]

This is why we're beginning this practical book on the subject of changing your habits from the inside out—by renewing your mind. We both have experienced the powerful and profound difference that thoughts have in our lives. We know that if we can partner the best techniques for transforming the mind with the most effective strategies to develop lean, healthy bodies and fat wallets, we have a terrific chance of acquiring lasting success in both areas of life!

> We are what we repeatedly do; excellence then is not an act, but a habit.
>
> —Aristotle

The You Are What You Think Habit

The most important habit is the You Are What You Think Habit. In fact, this is a foundational habit to the other three habits you will learn about in upcoming chapters. Here's a reality we sometimes fail to recognize: most people know *what* they need to do to live more productive, successful lives. The real problem is that they don't know *how* to do those things consistently and permanently.

In the area of money, who doesn't understand that spending more money than you have creates debt? And almost everyone knows if you eat more calories than you burn, you'll gain weight. Nevertheless, this knowledge is rarely enough to motivate most people to change. Simple self-discipline is not so simple. Many of us give up because we cannot figure out *how* to get ourselves to practice new behaviors consistently enough to reap lasting rewards.

By understanding that your habitual, dominant thoughts drive your emotions and behavior, you can begin to change your bad habits by changing how you think. This is the most effective way to realize lasting and dynamic change. When you couple new, healthy habits of the mind with effective daily practices, you will experience amazing results.

Since it takes time to rewire your brain effectively, we will give you simple steps to move you toward your goals both internally—in your thoughts—as well as externally—in your behaviors. The objective is for your external behaviors to become your new "autopilot." If you follow this plan, you'll likely want to incorporate many of these life-changing principles into other areas of your life as well.

For years, behavioral psychologists have said that it takes about twenty-one days to change a habit. With the advances in brain science, we now understand that at about twenty-one days, the neuron pathways in the brain begin to change. If an old dominant message is ignored, the neuron pathway will start to shrink. If a new message is repeated day after day, it will start to grow. The old and new messages don't change places at twenty-one days; the neuron pathways simply *begin* to respond to the new input. It is essential to understand that for unhealthy thoughts to lose their power, you must squelch those thoughts and replace them with new, healthy ones day after day.

Self-Talk Success

Almost twenty years ago, I (Danna) heard a life story that Shad Helmstetter, PhD, shared about his personal battle with being over-weight and how he finally realized lasting success. Helmstetter is the best-selling author of thirteen books on personal growth, self-talk, self-esteem, personal programming, and goal setting. He explained that he had been significantly overweight for many years, trying one diet after another. In fact, he became very good at losing weight, but he was equally adept at gaining it back . . . and then some. In his personal research about high-performance athletes, he discovered that some Eastern European

Olympians had full-time self-talk trainers who helped them develop new messages to drive them toward optimal levels of performance. Apparently, the results were significant, and this intrigued Helmstetter. Since those athletes significantly improved their performance and actually won gold medals, perhaps he could shed his unwanted pounds once and for all.

Shad decided to try this method on his battle of the bulge. He wrote detailed scripts related to healthy eating and living and had them professionally recorded in a studio. When the cassette tapes arrived, he began listening to them every morning while he shaved at his bathroom mirror. Amazingly, over a ten-week period, Dr. Helmstetter lost thirty-eight pounds—and he never gained them back. More amazingly, his wife, who was putting on her makeup at the same bathroom counter, lost twenty-five pounds by eavesdropping on his self-talk messages![3]

When I heard this story, some of the dramatic changes that had occurred in my life—my ability to overcome panic attacks as well as the lasting victory I'd won over emotional eating—started to make logical sense. I had been practicing healthy self-talk for years without knowing what to label it. I replaced my old destructive messages such as, *I can't stop eating. I'm losing my mind. I'll never lose weight*, with more constructive ones such as, *I am in control of my food choices. I can eat small amounts and be satisfied. My mind is strong, and I am not afraid.* I learned to tell myself the truth and refused to dwell on the lies I'd been telling myself for too long.

After a few months of repeating new messages, I noticed my cravings for food and my sense of panic were less intense. Then the frequency of my anxiety attacks and binge eating diminished. After one year, the panic attacks were gone—permanently. Over time, I gained total victory over not only my bulimic behavior but my emotional eating altogether.

In my (Ellie's) case, Bob and I needed to change our mind-sets to desire being debt-free more than enjoying daily indulgences that increased our debt and stress. By working together on the habits you will learn in this book, we realized some amazing financial rewards with Bob on a military man's salary while I was a stay-at-home mom. Fifteen years later, we have paid cash for eleven cars, given away three of those, bought two homes, and regularly taken family vacations. In the process, our kids got to wear "cool" clothes, and we supported more than thirty nonprofit organizations in a dozen different countries around the world. On top of that, all our children are on track to graduate from college debt-free, and Bob and I have a nice nest egg for retirement and a home that will be completely paid for upon retirement. Through practicing these habits consistently, we discovered an attainable and sustainable lifestyle that has promoted security, generosity, and many positive material rewards.

Practice Makes Permanent

You've probably heard and even used the cliché "Practice makes perfect." However, an observation attributed to teacher Alexander Liberman and others is more accurate: "Practice makes permanent." Whatever we practice continually will become ingrained in our neuron pathways. Being intentional about our mental habits is essential if we want to reach our most important goals and live with greater power and purpose.

> Watch your thoughts—they become your words.

> Watch your words—they become your actions.

> Watch your actions—they become your habits.

> Watch your habits—they become your character.

> Watch your character—it determines your destiny.

Simple Steps to Change Your Mind

The concept of the You Are What You Think Habit is simple. Yet many people don't know how to implement healthy thinking in a practical and time-efficient way. That is the ultimate purpose of this book—showing you how to implement simple strategies to change your habits in a new and lasting way. The four steps below will help you start building a new, strong, and positive habit.

STEP #1: IDENTIFY THE LIES YOU BELIEVE

The first step in transforming your thinking is to identify some of the thoughts or beliefs that underlie your unhealthy habits. We call those "lies." For example, if you find it difficult to stay on a budget and tend to overspend and run up your lines of credit, you may be telling yourself messages such as, *I deserve this indulgence. I work hard.* Or perhaps you say, *Who knows what tomorrow will bring? I might as well spend my savings now.* You many not say these things out loud. Most people are not tuned in to their inner messages. One of the easiest ways to identify unhealthy thoughts is to work backward by writing down the behaviors you want to change. So let's get started with a simple exercise.

First, list one or more behaviors you would like to change. Next to that entry, write the rationalization/lie you think you may be using that relates to that behavior. For example:

Behavior to Change	Rationalization/Lie
Spending too much money at department stores	*When I look good, I feel good.*
Eating too much at night after dinner	*I can't control my cravings. I deserve this.*

Now it's your turn. Spend a few minutes thinking about why you picked up this book in the first place. First, list the behaviors you want to change. Then jot down what you think may be the underlying thought that drives you toward that behavior.

Behavior to Change	Rationalization/Lie

It doesn't matter if you cannot fully define the lie at first. Just recognize that your strong, negative habits are being pushed by strong, negative thoughts. As you become more mindful of your thought life and evaluate your feelings related to the behavior you want to change, you'll begin to understand your underlying motivations.

According to Dr. Archibald Hart, former dean of the graduate school of psychology at Fuller Theological Seminary and author of *Habits of the Mind*,

Some thoughts are voluntary, we intentionally originate them. We choose to deliberately think about them. Others are involuntary and not necessarily welcome. Sometimes they intrude into our awareness like a burglar coming to rob us of our peace of mind. Other times they stay hidden, waiting to attack until they can achieve their damaging effects. As if they have a mind of their own, they intrude at the most inopportune times.

A healthy mind must have the skill to reduce the influence of these uncontrolled thoughts. We do this by making sure they are always out in the open, deliberately keeping them in our conscious awareness. They are easier to control and cannot do the same amount of damage when we are able to stare them straight in the face as they speak to us.[4]

Keep a Thought Notebook. An expert in cognitive therapy, stress management, and overcoming bad habits, Dr. Hart recommends that you become more aware of your negative thinking by keeping a small notebook nearby to record what you are thinking and feeling when negative emotions or actions rear their ugly heads. You can also use your smartphone to alert you to do an occasional reality check on your thinking throughout the day and record any recent negative self-talk.

Some negative emotions are necessary and accurate. For example, if you've done something that you know is wrong, feeling guilty is an appropriate response. Hopefully, that will help you act in a way that brings restitution or restoration and prompt you to act appropriately the next time. These types of negative emotions can influence you toward a better path. You don't need to change them. However, many chronic harmful emotions are the result of untruths inflicted on us by others. We hear them for so long that we believe them. As a result, we may not be aware of our actual thought stream from negative thought to negative emotion to negative action.

Follow the Trail of Persistent Negative Emotions. We can become so accustomed to our negative thinking that we are unaware of the undesirable thoughts we need to erase and replace. Another clue to discovering harmful thought patterns is to follow the trail of persistent negative emotions. Behind each persistent negative emotion is an underlying thought. Ask yourself, "What does this feeling or action say about what I think?"

If you are experiencing chronic angry emotions, you are thinking a lot of angry thoughts. If you are experiencing chronic insecurity, you're likely making diminishing comments about yourself. Chronically frustrated? Yep, you're right—you are probably dwelling on things that frustrate you. Whatever the persistent emotion, there is a strong thought pathway dug like a deep groove in your neuron pathways that has become a superhighway in your brain leading you down a path of emotions and actions that feel out of your control.

Lest you get depressed and try to suppress all your emotions, please remember that persistent positive and delightful emotions work in the opposite, positive direction. When you dwell on positive things and adopt an attitude of gratitude, welcomed emotions that enrich your life follow!

Record Your Emotions. Our emotions are simply responders to our thoughts. They are often more honest than the lies that are hiding beneath the surface, too ugly to be named. In your thought notebook, you can start recording emotions as well and jot down the thoughts you think may be the driving force behind them. Becoming more aware of your undesirable emotions and thinking allows you to take the next step toward changing your mind.

STEP #2: TAKE YOUR NEGATIVE THOUGHTS CAPTIVE

As you begin to identify more clearly the most dominant lies that are supporting your unhealthy habits, your assignment is to squash those thoughts and move to the next step. We call this "taking negative thoughts captive." Imagine each unwanted thought (or emotion that hints at those thoughts) like a thief entering your home and attempting to rob you of your most prized possessions. In this case, the thief of unhealthy thoughts steals the joy and power in your life. But you have the weapon to stop the invasion by simply redirecting your thoughts. Learn to recognize unhealthy thoughts quickly and refuse to dwell on them. You have much more control over your thoughts than you realize, and it will get stronger as you start to move consistently through these steps on a regular basis.

Review Your Thoughts and Emotions. Over the next week or so, review the notes you make in your thought notebook and ask yourself these questions:

1. What are the dominant negative messages I seem to repeat most often?
2. Is there a theme to those messages?
3. What negative emotions do I experience most often?
4. What do these emotions say about my underlying thoughts?

Write these questions in your notebook and refer to them often until you are clear which thoughts need permanent erasing. When they bubble to the surface, take them captive immediately.

Caution: Stop Thinking Now! Imagine the negative emotions you experience as flashing yellow lights alerting you to take caution before they prompt you to action. Negative thoughts and their resulting actions should be seen as flashing red lights with a loud siren projecting the most important message for that moment: *stop!*

STEP #3: CONSTRUCT NEW THOUGHTS TO COUNTERACT THE LIES

Developing healthy thoughts to replace your lies is essential to your success. There are specific exercises included throughout this book to help you design new messages. We've also included personal evaluations worded in such a way that you can use the statements as positive self-talk. Using your thought notebook, record healthy statements that will help you counteract the lies you believe. You can add to this list or modify statements as you become more self-aware.

Additionally, we have found that listening to healthy self-talk CDs is an effective and simple way to transform your mind. I (Danna) have used these for almost twenty years to help my clients and readers transform their habits. We have produced a new CD specific to establishing productive thinking in the area of both health and wealth called *Lean Bodies . . . Fat Wallets Self-Talk.*[5] It is designed to help you focus on universally helpful key statements that will diminish unproductive attitudes about your body or finances and replace them with statements that will drive you toward healthier habits.

STEP #4: REPEAT YOUR HEALTHY SELF-TALK UNTIL NEW DOMINANT THOUGHTS FORM

Identifying and writing down your healthy self-talk is not enough. In order for those thought messages to make a lasting impact on your behavior, you need to repeat them until new, dominant thoughts form. There are two stages to this process. The first is what we call top-of-the-mind awareness. By listening to healthy self-talk CDs or saying your new statements aloud several times a day, you are bringing them into your conscious thinking. Much like a song that repeats in your mind all day long after hearing it on the radio, your messages repeated during the day start to pop to the surface without conscious thought.

Using your thought notebook and intentionally becoming mindful of your negative thoughts keeps you focused on the You Are What You Think Habit. It's like buying a new car. Suddenly you see your same model everywhere. The number of those cars on the road hasn't changed, but your awareness of them has. Additionally, saying your self-talk messages out loud will enhance the benefits of your new self-talk. Always end your day by making your final conscious thoughts intentional and productive. You can do this by leaving a few of your key thoughts on index cards on your bedside table. Make it a nightly habit to read them (preferably out loud) just before turning off your light.

The second and most important part of this step takes much longer—changing your actual, physical neuron pathways. As we mentioned earlier, this process doesn't even *begin* to take place physiologically until about twenty-one days of consistent, repeated self-talk. As with building a house, simply laying the foundation does not make it a dwelling. The frame must be erected one board at a time. Then the windows, doors, flooring, and other finishing work must be completed before you can move in and call it a home. As you build the foundation of a healthy mind-set, remember that your new messages won't become dominant overnight. Keep building them day after day, week after week, month after month.

If you are consistent, you will begin to notice subtle shifts in your attitudes, emotions, and behavior. In the past, you likely had to muster significant self-control in the most tempting of situations. Soon you will notice it is easier to say no to your impulses. When you start to notice a new empowerment, don't stop practicing healthy self-talk! Most of us have been listening to the old messages for many years and need to reinforce our new thoughts long after we start to experience positive changes. When you get your teeth filled and are cavity-free, you don't stop brushing your teeth. Your new healthy self-talk is a daily habit you need to practice to keep a "cavity free" brain for the rest of your life! As you learn to speak truth into your health and wealth habits, you can use these same principles in many other areas of your life.

Use Triggering Events. Like practicing bedtime self-talk, you can use other triggering events to make Step #4 a deeply engrained habit. One type of trigger is a negative, inciting emotion or behavior. Whenever you feel negative emotions, such as frustration, lack of self-control, sadness, loneliness, or anger, turn them into reminders to take your lies captive and replace them with healthy self-talk.

When I (Danna) was battling with persistent panic attacks, I began to use my fear to trigger healthy self-talk. My old messages were: *I'm losing my mind. I'm freaking out and I'm going to make a fool of myself any minute. If I can't get it together, I may have a mental breakdown. I probably am having a breakdown right now. If I'm not mentally ill, I likely have a brain tumor causing all this. Most tumors are cancer. I must have brain cancer. Oh my word, I could be dying. I wonder how long I have to live.*

This type of stream of thought was my abnormal norm. It's no wonder I was an exhausted, emotional wreck. I started to see my impending panic attack as that yellow caution light we mentioned earlier and used it as a trigger to tell myself the truth such as, *I am in control of my thoughts. I have a sound mind and not a spirit of fear. I am able to relax and let go of my anxiety.*

Another type of trigger is one you choose to use as a reminder to practice healthy self-talk throughout the day, such as brushing your teeth, starting your car, or any number of other mundane tasks. Choose something you do numerous times a day as your trigger and multitask toward healthier self-talk!

Evaluate and Change Your Thoughts. One easy way to identify negative thinking is by taking a personal evaluation. We have prepared separate health and wealth tests below for this purpose. As we already mentioned, they are worded in a positive fashion and give you an excellent model for replacing your old negative messages with healthier ones. Once you've taken the tests, we'll tell you how to do just that.

Health Attitudes

Rate yourself based on the last six to twelve months as follows:
0—Almost never; 1—Sometimes; 2—Often; 3—Always

_____ I like my body and feel good about myself most days.

_____ I am in control of my lifestyle choices and make healthy choices most days.

_____ I have a positive attitude about life and feel all things are possible.

_____ When I set my mind to something, I take action and follow through.

_____ I enjoy physical activity and crave exercise.

_____ I am in control of my habits; they are not in control of me.

_____ I am aware of my negative self-talk and make efforts to replace it.

_____ I believe I can and will change my unhealthy habits.

_____ I choose to eat healthfully and enjoy nutritious foods.

_____ I am grateful for what I have and who I am.

_____ I appreciate others and both give and receive support when needed.

_____ Overall, I am content with my body and my life.

_____ My goals for my body and health are realistic and attainable.

_____ I give myself grace when I mess up and get back on track quickly.

_____ I can see myself making healthy changes permanently.

_____ I rarely make excuses for my health problems but take responsibility and action.

How Did You Score?

40–48   Excellent! You seem to have a good handle on your attitude.

31–39   Good. Your thinking is pretty good, but there's room for improvement.

22–30   Fair. It's definitely time to take action and ditch the unhealthy self-talk.

< 21   Poor. Take one step at a time and begin taking action today.

Wealth Attitudes

Rate yourself based on the last six to twelve months as follows:
0—Almost never; 1—Sometimes; 2—Often; 3—Always

_____   I like my home/clothes/furniture and feel good about my material assets most days.

_____   I am in control of my spending habits and make smart financial decisions most days.

_____   I am energized about digging out of consumer debt and feel all things are possible.

_____   When I set my mind to save money, I take action and follow through.

_____   I enjoy living within my means and sharing my abundance with others.

_____   I manage my money in ways that support future security.

_____   I am aware of my negative self-talk about my material assets, job, and finances and make efforts to keep these areas healthy.

_____   I believe I can and will change my unhealthy fiscal habits.

_____   My self-control in curbing impulse buys is strong.

_____ I appreciate the needs of the less fortunate and give of my time and material goods in order to help others.

_____ Overall, I am content with my money and my life.

_____ My goals for my wealth are realistic and attainable.

_____ I give myself grace when I mess up on my budget and get back on track quickly.

_____ I can see myself making healthy fiscal changes permanently.

_____ I rarely make excuses for my financial problems but take responsibility and action.

How Did You Score?

40–48   Excellent! You seem to have a good handle on your attitude.

31–39   Good. Your thinking is pretty good, but there's room for improvement.

22–30   Fair. It's definitely time to take action and ditch the unhealthy self-talk.

< 21   Poor. Take one step at a time and begin taking action today.

Take Action

One of the best ways to take immediate action is to circle the statements where you rated yourself the lowest. You can use these positive comments to begin erasing and replacing your negative self-talk. Transfer these to your thought notebook and also put a few of the most important statements on index cards. Read these several times each day. Better yet, memorize them and create a trigger event that reminds you to say them all day long. Follow the timeless advice of Nike—Just Do It!

The illiterate individual of the future will not be the person who does not know how to read but the person who does not know how to think.

—Archibald Hart, PhD

But Wait . . . There's More!

One Friday this past fall, I (Danna) sat among thousands of business people at a huge corporate conference overloaded with information and wishing it was time to go back to my hotel room and get some much-needed rest. And then a somewhat nerdy, thirty-something guy named Shawn Achor stepped on the stage and captivated my attention for over an hour with his fresh and energetic teaching on positive psychology. This young PhD graduate from Harvard shared lots of information about the power of our thoughts—information that I was studying, writing, and teaching about probably before he graduated from high school. I was familiar with the well-documented science behind the physiology of the brain and its ability to change. But what was exciting to me was the validation in his book, *The Happiness Advantage,* that developing new internal wiring not only changes our emotions and redirects our behavior but also significantly impacts our happiness.[6]

You Can Be Happy!

Despite the fact that Shawn's book was primarily written to help organizations develop more productive employees, its content is a must-read for anyone who wants to better understand the simple principles for becoming a more positive and productive person. Let's face it, becoming content with our day-to-day lives is the underlying reason that so many of us strive to reach goals like losing weight, dumping our debt, or acquiring more wealth. If we could learn to become more content—especially with things that are out of our control—wouldn't that be worth pursuing?

Shawn's research validated that we can almost *immediately* influence our contentment and productivity by learning to practice a few simple habits. For example, by watching a funny video clip or thinking about something that brings you great joy before taking on a challenging task (like taking an exam or writing an important business letter), you can enhance your performance at that task and even your enjoyment while doing it. This is just another layer of understanding that will hopefully encourage you to commit yourself to a lifetime of developing an intentional, proactive You Are What You Think Habit in every area of your life!

3.

The 3D Habit

*Overcome temptation by applying the
three basic principles of this habit.*

In ages past, it was much more difficult to satisfy our cravings and urges. There were no fast-food restaurants or all-night minimarts to which we could sneak out at any hour and load ourselves up with junk food galore. There were no shopping malls or endless selection of specialty shops where we could shop to our heart's content. And there certainly was not television to tempt us with tantalizing commercials or access to the worldwide web where we could exercise our need for retail therapy 24/7. Yes, in simpler times it was much easier to avoid temptation.

A Temptation Deterrent Strategy

When my (Danna's) client Sheri lost twenty-five pounds, she was delighted. Since January, she'd consistently practiced basic small steps toward her goal. She ate about 150 calories less each day and burned about 200 calories more and watched the pounds slowly melt off and stay off over an eleven-month period. It was hard to believe that such small changes could add up in such a significant way. Now, with the holidays looming, Sheri was worried about the temptations that would be bombarding her at parties, buffets, office treats, and special dinners. Would she be able to withstand the pressure? I decided this was the perfect time to teach her the 3D Habit and help her safely negotiate through the holidays without gaining a single pound.

The 3D Habit: Determine—Distract—Delay

This habit is an excellent temptation deterrent strategy to help you navigate the frequent impulses we all encounter from time to time. This habit is described with three Ds that are easy to remember. Each stands for an important and effective strategy for changing your bad habits into healthy ones: *determine—distract—delay.*

Whenever you realize that you are going to be in a situation that may challenge your resolve to stick to your new health or financial plan, *determine* beforehand how you are going to handle it. Rather than just respond to situations as they emerge, give some forethought to common and occasional circumstances that may test you. You can practice new strategies to *distract* yourself from the temptation and to *delay* gratification until the time you decide is appropriate in light of your desired goal.

HEALTH AND THE 3D HABIT

Let's use Sheri as an example of practicing the three Ds in a common area of temptation—food—and in this case, a holiday buffet. Sheri knew that the scrumptious spread at the party would be calling her name, so Sheri *determined* beforehand to eat a small, healthy snack before the party. This would prevent her from experiencing low blood sugar or hunger that could weaken her resolve to eat less food and make healthier choices. She also determined to count calories, with a goal of having no more than six hundred calories during the party. Sheri practiced the next two Ds of *distracting* and *delaying* herself from over-eating by reconnecting with friends in the living room and engaging in meaningful conversations away from the buffet table. She told her-self that she could indulge in her plan of consuming her six hundred calories anytime she wanted, but in order to build up some of her self-control muscles, she would *delay* at least thirty minutes before tasting anything. Forty-five minutes later, she was still engrossed in conver-sations that completely took her mind off the food. She learned that following a *determined* plan, practicing *delay* strategies, and finding meaningful *distractions* were very helpful.

The 3D Habit is effective in dealing with every type of eating temp-tation. By determining to prepare in advance for situations that will be difficult, you can have a strategy to delay gratification and distract your-self from the foods that are calling your name. Below are a few common scenarios where you can use the 3D Habit.

TV or Movie Time

Determine to have a healthy meal two to three hours before your TV or movie time so you are not hungry when you sit down to watch. If you've planned to have a snack, bring/make your own lighter version of movie popcorn or try something like beef jerky or hard candy that lasts longer and delivers fewer calories. *Delay* indulging in your treat until the show starts. Also try to stop munching for five-minute intervals. This helps you build your self-control muscles and also learn to separate the enjoyment of watching from eating food. Try something new and *distract* yourself from eating at all the next time you watch a show. Pay extra attention to the music, creative techniques, quality of acting, or the storyline. In other words, get deeply engaged in what you are watching rather than diminishing the experience with the diversion of food.

End-of-the-Day Temptations

At the end of a long day, it is easy to rationalize all sorts of unhealthy behavior. When you are hungry, tired, stressed, or frustrated, you can easily throw caution to the wind and eat as a way to unwind and reward yourself. Unfortunately, there is also a price to pay that will diminish your health and increase your size. Instead, *determine* that you will have a plan to deal with end-of-the-day temptations. *Delay* succumbing to fast food, fattening snacks, or happy-hour indulgences at the end of the day by always having a healthy mid- to late-afternoon treat. Carry portion-controlled baggies of nuts, fruit, veggies, or even jerky. Make sure these snacks have a good source of protein and/or fiber to help stabilize your blood sugar. Include a full glass of water (sparkling is fine and filling if you like it) or a cup of herbal tea (hot or cold). This will ensure you are well hydrated and also diminish any residual hunger.

Now that you have dealt with hunger and energy, it is time to practice the art of distraction. *Distract* yourself from using food to relax or reward yourself by trying some new and healthier methods. For example, kick off your shoes and take a power nap. Or put on your favorite music, close your eyes, and simply relax and let your imagination wander. Need more ideas? Engage in a favorite hobby, take a long shower or bath, go for a walk, or call a friend. Practice finding creative distractions that feed your soul rather than your fat cells.

Dining Out

Eating dinner at a restaurant or as a guest at someone's home is often a stumbling block for those who are trying to take the small steps needed to lose weight or get healthier. Don't panic. Instead, use the 3D Habit strategically. You can *determine* to address several key issues beforehand. First, determine to have a healthy attitude and realize that one meal will not be your undoing. Second, determine that you will not use your lack of total control over your choices as an excuse for caving in to every temptation. If you are going to a restaurant, determine beforehand what type of menu choices will help you best reach your goal, and then stick to those predetermined decisions. If you plan wisely, you will not arrive starving, so you can pass on the appetizers and *delay* taking your first bite until the main course is served. *Distract* yourself by choosing to talk more and eat less—engaging in conversation and the satisfaction of connecting with others more than food. Then practice the *delay* strategy one more time and pass on dessert. If you know the people you are dining with well, take one small bite of their dessert and practice this healthy self-talk message: *I am easily satisfied with a small taste of rich foods and desserts.* If you do this each time you are presented with these types of temptations, you'll discover the 3D Habit will becomes your new normal.

> Start where you are and do what you can. The only failure is to do nothing at all.
>
> —Ellie Kay

WEALTH AND THE 3D HABIT

Samantha was a chronic shopaholic who was a sucker for a bargain even when those bargains threw her off budget. Since she was single and didn't have the accountability of a husband who shared the debt and frustration of a growing credit card bill, it was easy to live for the moment and worry about the money later. After attending one of Ellie's financial seminars, she decided to apply the 3D Habit to her spending practices. Here is what her process looked like:

Determine to Be Accountable

Samantha decided that making herself accountable to her best friend, Katherine, would help her stop impulse shopping. Her friend agreed to call her once a week and ask her what bargains she bought online, at the mall, or on her phone.

Distract from Impulse Buying

When Samantha encountered an irresistible bargain, red sale tag, or 20-percent-off savings, she took a few seconds to text her friend: "I'm being tempted." She also chose to focus her mind on her new goal of paying off her debt and thought, *If I don't spend twenty dollars on this bargain, that's twenty dollars I can put toward my Visa bill.* These tactics were effective enough to distract her from the impulse to spend.

Delay before Purchasing

If the item really was a bargain, she truly needed it, *and* it was within her budget, she took a photo of the item, noted the day the sale ended, and sent herself a calendar alert to reconsider the purchase before that date. She said that nine times out of ten, this final habit of *delay* was sufficient enough to help her see that even though the item was a bargain and within her budget, she didn't really need it and could pass on it when she had the benefit of time and space away from the impulse urge.

The Payoff of the 3D Habit

When Samantha first began the 3D Habit, it felt awkward and cumbersome. After all, she felt a little odd making herself accountable and texting her friend when she was tempted to make a purchase. But she was determined to pay off her consumer debt and build a cash reserve. She said, "The temporary discomfort involved in breaking a bad habit was replaced by the permanent joy of reaching my financial goal." In fact, her accountability friend noticed the transformation in Samantha's spending habits and decided to apply this effective new habit to her desire to become more physically active. Katherine developed a new habit of walking three times a week in the process. Both friends are happier, healthier, and wealthier due to the mutual accountability they applied to the 3D Habit.

It is easy to apply this habit to all aspects of your financial life, from learning to be content with the money you currently make, to being able to stick to your family budget. By practicing what the late Stephen Covey taught in *The 7 Habits of Highly Effective People* and "beginning with the end in mind," you can go a long way toward recognizing the value of implementing the 3D Habit into your daily life every time a temptation arises that veers you off course.[1]

The 3D Habit Applied to Long-Term Financial Goals

If one of your financial goals is to go on vacation debt-free (we will discuss frugal vacations in chapter 9), then that objective can help you resist the urge to buy your seven-year-old daughter an American Girl doll dress because she wants it, she's cute, and you want to make her happy. Instead, you *determine* that your overriding goal is more important than an optional item that isn't going to get you to that debt-free vacation. You choose to *distract* yourself (and her) by saying, "It's not in the budget" and *delay* the urge by adding, "You have plenty of other outfits for your doll. Let's go try some new combinations of her wardrobe to create new looks."

FROM HABIT TO PHILOSOPHY

A lot of Americans want to live healthier and wealthier lives, but they don't know how to get there. When you decide to follow the 3D Habit as a bigger part of your life philosophy, it can transform the way you approach both health and wealth in powerful ways. For example, you may want to think through ways to use this habit to create an overriding philosophy that serves as a guide to making all health and wealth decisions.

Wealth Philosophy

Most people who have a lot of money know that it does not emotionally satisfy a human being. Each of us must determine how we will choose to define success apart from monetary wealth. The Money, Meaning, and Choices (MMC) Institute works with people who have achieved financial success and found that the "suddenly rich" have no place to explore matters of money and meaning.[2] In fact, many of these topics suddenly become taboo among friends and family of the nouveau riche. A typical response would be, "Oh, I should have *your* problems." The new status and emotions that accompany sudden wealth often distance the newly wealthy from the people who matter most to them.

As you determine what is truly important, decide in advance what you will measure as success. Does it mean that you earn a six-figure income? If this is your definition, you have defined yourself by what you make or acquire. Consider a healthier perspective such as, *I am a success because I find satisfaction in my work, treat others fairly, and maintain a good reputation.* That way, even if your company downsizes and you are suddenly underemployed or even unemployed, you've determined your worth and success based on things you can control.

Health Philosophy

In today's culture, it's easy to believe that your value as a person is directly related to your physical appearance. That is one of the reasons so many women struggle with eating disorders and become obsessed with extreme measures to stay looking youthful. *Determine* the philosophy you want to live by related to your health and appearance. There is no doubt that those who have good health (which includes maintaining a reasonable weight) can enjoy life more fully. But there are some things out of our control. If we constantly measure our value to Hollywood's standard, we will be miserable.

I (Danna) determined many years ago to adopt this philosophy about my health and appearance: *I will do the right things (eat, exercise, and live healthfully) for the right reasons (to enhance my overall health) and trust God with the results!* My point was to determine to focus on what I did have control over—my lifestyle choices—and let go of what I did not—the exact end result. I figured if I did my part, my "best" body would follow. Despite my fairly youthful appearance as a sixty-year-old woman, I am still aging. I've *determined* to accept what I cannot change and embrace every season of life.

A DELAY A DAY KEEPS POOR DECISIONS AT BAY

Make a life decision to practice the *delay* step of the 3D Habit as part of your normal way of life. Commit to delaying emotional indulgences even if only for a few minutes in order to ask yourself some defining questions before taking action. For example, "Does this purchase or food move me closer to my goal?" "Will I feel good about this decision an hour or day from now?" Commit to waiting a few minutes (before ordering the decadent dessert) or a few days (before signing for the red convertible). Practiced over and over, this strategy will become an ingrained habit that protects you from regret and helps you find creative ways of designing a lifestyle that is closely aligned with your core values and interests.

It's wise to remember this simple statement: "When in doubt, don't . . ." Instead of taking immediate action, *delay* what you've decided (in advance) in a wise time frame. Then, once that time has passed, decide if taking action is a wise choice.

DISTRACT YOURSELF—SQUIRREL!

Have you ever taken a walk with a hound dog? One second the dog is fixated on a smell in front of it; the next second it's off and running after a squirrel. Sometimes distractions can send us off track from our goals. But when we are intentional, distractions can protect us from our own bad habits. If habits like shopping or indulging in unhealthy foods are your challenges, find a few delightful "squirrels" to distract you from your bad habits. For example, when it comes to food temptations, a helpful distraction is to do something you enjoy that keeps you too busy to munch. In an ideal world, you would distract yourself from food by stepping away from the table, kitchen, or restaurant. To avoid unnecessary purchases, you would stay away from the mall, shopping channel, or your favorite website and choose to read a great book, take a walk with a friend, or some other quality diversion.

Unfortunately, you cannot always remove yourself from tempting environments, so you must learn how to create your own mental distractions. This strategy partners the You Are What You Think Habit with the 3D Habit. Develop a few key statements that become your go-to self-talk phrases for dealing with your most challenging and common temptations. Memorize and repeat these statements every day and always before and during the time you are facing a temptation. Here are a few examples you may want to use or modify:

- *I always take control of my urge to buy something and first consider my budget and my financial goals. I never make purchases that I have not predetermined are wise.*
- *I always decide beforehand what "fun foods" I will choose to include in my daily food choices. I have the strength to avoid any food that does not help me meet my goal.*
- *I can see a sale or product I've been wanting and delay a decision to purchase it on the spot. I find great satisfaction in saying no to spontaneous buying.*
- *I am in control of my food choices and can distract myself with conversation or other activities even when others are eating foods I chose not to eat.*

Instead of being distracted by material items that will never satisfy or foods that will make you feel fat and guilty later, distract yourself with your goals that help you live intentionally and with greater purpose. These positive distractions are ones that will keep you focused and help you make wise choices. All human beings long to discover spheres of interest that add meaning and passion to our lives. We'd like to believe we are here for a specific purpose beyond that of simply accumulating health and wealth.

Some people can achieve it all—the perfect body and exceeding wealth—and yet discover that they are not satisfied. On the other hand, there are others who seem to have very little and never reach their ideal weight, yet have learned to be content because they live with an abundance mentality. George Bernard Shaw put it well when he wrote his opening words to the play *Man and Superman:*

This is the true joy in life, the being used for a purpose recognized by yourself as a mighty one; the being thoroughly worn out before you are thrown on the scrap heap; the being a force of nature instead of a feverish selfish little clod of ailments and grievances complaining that the world will not devote itself to making you happy.[3]

No one can make you content but you. Your spouse cannot, neither can your preacher or your friend. Mother Teresa said, "Do not wait for leaders. Do it alone, person to person."[4] She was referring to the wealth of purpose as demonstrated by where you put your time, efforts, and resources. The most content people are not those who have acquired perfect bodies or amassed great wealth, but rather those who have found true purpose. When we discover our God-given purpose and help others do the same, our lives are richer and more rewarding. By being good stewards of what God has given us physically and materially, we can make intentional deposits that satisfy us for a lifetime. Make a decision—*determine*—to follow this 3D Habit, and you will find yourself healthy and wealthy in the things that matter most.

Take Action

In the space below, write down one or two scenarios in which you are tempted to overindulge or pursue immediate gratification rather than your ultimate goals. Under each scenario, jot down a couple of ideas next to each of the three Ds that may help you find new strength to choose the better path the next time you're feeling lured into a poor choice.

Scenario #1:	
Determine:	
Delay:	
Distract:	
Scenario #2:	
Determine:	
Delay:	
Distract:	

4.

The In and Out Habit

*Learn the power of a reality check and
make wiser choices with this habit.*

Debby cringed as the nurse announced her weight to everyone within earshot. In one short year, since her last annual exam, she had gained five pounds. Five pounds was not a big deal . . . except for the fact that she had gained five each year for the last four years and now was twenty pounds overweight. How could this be happening? She'd been exercising at least three to four times a week for years. She rarely ate desserts and usually avoided bread and extra helpings at meals. In fact, she was pretty sure she ate less now than she did when she was a teenager.

The Four-Cracker Factor

Debby did eat less than she used to, but she also was much less active. She had no idea that on average, she ate about fifty calories per day more than she was burning. That tiny amount—the equivalent of four saltine crackers—was the reason she was carrying excess weight. If she did not take the time to do a reality check and learn to be mindful of her In and Out Habit, she'd likely put on another twenty pounds by the time she turned fifty.

Statistically, most people gain twenty-five pounds between the ages of thirty and fifty by only eating five to ten calories per day more than they burn. Small, unaccounted-for morsels of food can add up. Debby didn't want to be another statistic.

Five Dollars a Day Keeps the Sports Car Away

A typical bachelor, Steve rushes out of the house each morning without breakfast and makes a quick stop at his favorite coffee shop for a large espresso and breakfast sandwich. He's a busy guy and figures this small expenditure is no big deal. What he doesn't realize is that his five-dollar daily purchase has added up to $9,100 over the past five years.

He's also been spending a bit more than he makes each month, so some purchases are floating on his credit card bill. By maintaining an unpaid balance of about $3,000 over five years with a relatively low interest rate of 8 percent, Steve's paid an additional $1,200 for his daily breakfast habit, which now totals over $10,000! If he'd been mindful of all his other small purchases that were "no big deal," he could have saved enough for a sizable down payment on the sports car he'd been wishing he could afford since he graduated from college. Sports car or coffee? Steve *could* have chosen the car if he'd realized how paying attention to the In and Out Habit would have helped him achieve his goal.

> Healthy habits are not a thing of chance but of choice. As with any bad habit, a new and healthier habit can be practiced so as to replace a bad one.
>
> —Caroline Leaf, PhD

In Versus Out

Everyone knows that if you eat more calories than you burn, you will gain weight. Similarly, no one would argue that if you spend more money than you make, you will soon find yourself in deep debt. Yet too many people live as if these simple realities were not true. That's because little indulgences and expenditures seem harmless. But they add up in big ways over time!

Being aware of your intake versus output all day long is a habit worth forming. Paying attention to the details can either make you or break you. Most people err greatly when "guesstimating" their intake of calories or expenditures. Gaining awareness of these details can turn the tables favorably on your lifestyle. Just imagine being debt-free. Can you see yourself lean and feeling fit? The In and Out Habit, partnered with the other habits you've been learning, will help you make small daily choices that will deliver big rewards.

In this chapter, we will ask you to consider your intake versus output in our respective areas of expertise. In later chapters, we will give you specific strategies to implement that will help you move your in-versus-out equations in the right direction.

HEALTH AND THE IN AND OUT HABIT

It seems a new weight-loss diet hits the market almost every month. Yet the obesity epidemic continues to soar. For the last sixteen years, I (Danna) have been teaching and writing that the most important factor related to weight loss is "calories in versus calories out." It isn't so much *what* you eat, but how much. Most health experts, including the mainstream medical community, have supported this well-documented premise for decades despite the apparent endless "new discoveries" about weight loss that promise lasting breakthroughs. Unfortunately, according to the International Food Information Council (IFIC), their 2012 Food and Health Survey concluded that fewer than 10 percent of Americans correctly estimate the number of calories they need to lose or maintain their weight.[1]

Research published in the *New England Journal of Medicine* confirmed once again the importance of calorie reduction for weight loss. In their two-year study, 811 overweight participants were assigned to one of four reduced-calorie diets with different combinations of protein, carbohydrates, and fats. The results revealed that from a weight-loss perspective, it didn't matter what foods the participants ate but how many calories they consumed.[2]

This is not to say that the type and ratio of fats, proteins, and carbohydrates don't matter. They do, but not as much as most people think. Even people who choose to eat all-natural, organic foods and never let a speck of sugar or white flour touch their lips can be overweight—*if* they eat more calories than they burn. The good news for those folks is that most people don't overindulge as excessively on healthy foods!

The In and Out Habit also applies to the quality of the calories we are ingesting. What we put in produces what we put out (and I'm not speaking of poop!). You cannot build a brick house out of straw, nor can you build a healthy body out of French fries and cheeseburgers. We need to give our bodies quality building materials in order to maintain healthy bodies. At this writing, I (Danna) just turned sixty, yet I am regularly mistaken for being in my midforties. A little hair color helps—but I am lean, fit, and high energy because I follow the In and Out Habit in the area of my nutrition and calories very consistently. As you already read, this wasn't always true. Thankfully, we can reverse years of unhealthy living by practicing healthier habits consistently.

So how do you think you are doing managing your In and Out Habit? Are you burning more calories than you eat? Are you eating more healthy foods than junk foods? If you're reading this section, I'm guessing you may need some help. The short evaluation that follows will give you some insight into the specific areas where you may need to be more mindful of this habit.

Nutrition and Exercise Habits

Rate yourself based on the last six to twelve months as follows:
0—Almost never; 1—Sometimes; 2—Often; 3—Always

_____ I know exactly how many calories I eat each day.

_____ I have a general concept of how many calories I eat each day.

_____ I read labels and am mindful of portions and total caloric value in foods.

_____ I know how many calories I burn most days.

_____ I maintain a very active lifestyle.

_____ I exercise aerobically four or more days every week.

_____ I generally eat only when I'm hungry.

_____ I rarely eat past mild fullness.

_____ I rarely eat two hours before bedtime.

_____ I limit desserts and empty calories to less than 10 percent of my daily diet.

_____ I eat seven to nine fruits and vegetables each day and mostly natural foods.

_____ I drink lots of purified water all day long.

_____ I limit my intake of saturated and trans fats.

_____ I eat to nourish my body more than I eat to satisfy my cravings.

_____ I am moderate with caffeine, alcohol, and sugar.

How Did You Score?

40–48   Excellent! You are feeding your body well, but not too much!

31–39   Good. Your nutritional habits are decent, but there's room for improvement.

22–30   Fair. It's time to decrease the unhealthy food and empty calories.

< 21   Poor. Take one step at a time and begin taking action today. You can do it!

Take Action

Take a few minutes to look back at your answers and circle the ones you rated less than "2." These are the lifestyle habits that most need your attention. Use the positive statements to improve your self-talk in these areas as you did with the earlier self-evaluation. You can also use the space below to choose your top three challenges and determine a more positive course of action. For example:

Key Statement #1: *I rarely eat two hours before bedtime.*   **Rating:** 0
My Plan: *I will start a new habit of not snacking two hours before bedtime and will drink herbal tea to satisfy my need to put something in my mouth. I will also look for positive distractions, such as a warm bath or good book instead of eating.*

Key Statement #1: _____ **Rating:** ____

My Plan: _____

Key Statement #2: _____ **Rating:** ____

My Plan: _____

Key Statement #3: _____ **Rating:** ____

My Plan: _____

WEALTH AND THE IN AND OUT HABIT

Spending more money than you make without concern for saving for the future is a formula that produces lots of stress and insecurity. It is one of the major reasons marriages fail and people live in a state of constant anxiety. Yet the solution is simple—stop unplanned spending. We totally understand that this is easier said than done. To implement the In and Out Habit effectively in your financial dimension, you need to get a reality check on exactly what you are spending and determine the best way to decrease the outgo of money. Most people who are struggling with too much debt run out of money before the end of the month because they don't pay close enough attention to their bottom line. In their case, ignorance is not bliss—it is a silent but deadly tsunami of rising debt and stress.

Newlywed Bliss

Jane and Doug were one of those blissful newlywed couples who did not worry about money during their first year of marriage. They believed the old adage that "two can live more cheaply than one." Since they were both working and now sharing a home, they had a false sense of confidence about their finances. They assumed they had more discretionary income than they really had. The problem was that they never took the time to compare their joint income to their expenses. They were so in love and caught up in the excitement of setting up their new life together that they used their credit cards far too often, figuring they would pay off the balance at the end of the month. But each month, the balance seemed a little too high to pay in one payment, so they paid a lower amount and intended to pay more the next month. Twelve months later, they wondered how they had maxed out their limits so quickly.

Not wanting to meddle, but responding to her daughter's lament about their predicament, Jane's mom shared a simple budget spreadsheet with Jane that helped her get a snapshot of their finances. Her mother had used a similar one for years and had not allowed their family to carry any revolving debt for at least a decade. In one column, they listed all the income that Jane and Doug could count on each month. Then they added a place to enter any potential bonuses or unexpected income. In another column, they listed all their monthly set expenses, such as rent, car payments, and insurance costs. Next, they listed variable expenses, such as utilities. Last, they set a budget for food, entertainment, discretionary spending, and savings. Jane was mortified when she realized that there was very little left for discretionary spending or entertainment. She showed Doug their financial picture, and they mutually decided to limit their entertainment and discretionary spending so they could pay off their credit card balances faster.

Once a week, Jane and Doug sat down together at their computer and input the past week's income and expenditures into their spreadsheet. They were able to make adjustments if needed. They also kept a list of all their debts and balances, celebrating with a preplanned dinner date every time they met a payoff goal. This new attention to the In and Out Habit gave Jane and Doug the exact information they needed to make wise choices. It was much more difficult to rationalize emotional/unbudgeted expenses when they both were so keenly aware of their bottom line.

Within eighteen months, this young couple was completely out of debt and on their way to developing a positive In and Out Habit that would not only help them financially but also help protect their marriage from becoming one more financially precipitated failure. In chapter 6, I will show you how to create a budget just like Jane and Doug's.

Dollars In Versus Dollars Out

Paying attention to the details in all areas of our finances can mean the difference between financial stability and bankruptcy. Just as a few extra calories can add up to a significant weight gain over several years, overspending a little more than three dollars per day can add up dangerously as well. Let's take a peek at exactly what a little extra spending can add up to over time:

Overspending

Year	Amount Overspent	Accumulated Interest	End of Year Balance
1	$1,200	$104	$1,304
2	1,200	463	2,863
3	1,200	1,128	4,728

Year	Amount Overspent	Accumulated Interest	End of Year Balance
4	1,200	2,157	6,957
5	1,200	3,621	9,621
6	1,200	5,608	12,808
7	1,200	8,217	16,617
8	1,200	11,572	21,172
9	1,200	15,818	26,618
10	1,200	21,129	33,129
11	1,200	27,714	40,914
12	1,200	35,821	50,221
13	1,200	45,749	61,349
14	1,200	57,855	74,655
15	1,200	72,562	90,562
TOTALS	$18,000	$72,562	$90,562

*Based on spending $100 over budget each month

This chart is a great reality check that can help you realize how those small, unplanned expenses only amounting to one hundred dollars per month can generate excessive debt over time. But what about other financial issues, such as buying a house or car? And how does the In and Out Habit address our need to finance our children's college educations? Taking the time each year to evaluate how much we have coming in versus how much we have going out can radically change the decisions we make and ensure a financially sound future.

5.

The Sustainable Lifestyle Habit

*Design a daily lifestyle of health and wealth
and still enjoy your life with this habit.*

The Quick-Fix Lifestyle

In 2007, John and Sally were excited to discover the house they purchased in 1997 had appreciated by $100,000. Over dinner one night, their neighbors, also thrilled about the booming house values, shared that they'd recently refinanced their home and taken a big chunk of equity to pay off all their credit cards and remodel their kitchen. Sally convinced her husband that this was the perfect solution to their $30,000 credit card debt, which had increased from $20,000 the year before. They knew they were paying way too much in interest rates and the task of paying off their bills felt daunting. As an added bonus, there would be enough equity left over to allow them to pull out some cash and make a down payment on the luxury car they'd been drooling over for the past two years. Once their monthly consumer debt was consolidated with a lower payment and interest rate, they would be motivated to stay debt-free, right? Wrong.

Within two years, John was totally stressed out trying to pay the increased mortgage debt on top of the consumer debt they had replenished, which now topped out at a whopping $35,000. Their value and equity in their home was significantly decreased to the point they were considered "underwater," which meant they owed more than the house was worth. On top of that, they had a car payment for the new luxury car that didn't seem nearly as "droolable" as it had the day they purchased it. What had seemed like a great plan for paying off debt morphed into a financial noose that was choking off their security and peace of mind.

The Drastic-Measures Lifestyle

Melissa was amazed at how much weight she was losing every week. After years of being obese, she decided to do something drastic and go on a strict liquid diet. She also hired a personal trainer and committed to taking on a rigorous workout schedule that included two hours of aerobic exercise—walking, swimming, or biking—and one hour of strength training seven days a week. Now, five months later, she'd lost sixty-five pounds and six sizes. For the first time in fifteen years, she slipped into a pair of size 8 jeans. She looked and felt amazing. Just ten pounds from her goal weight, she could almost count the days until she could chew food again and stop working out at such an intense pace.

Her husband, Ted, took her picture in a bathing suit on the day the scale declared she'd hit her goal. She'd never worked so hard for anything in her life. That was the last day her scale ever reported that weight. Slowly but surely, the numbers began to creep upward. She tried to eat low-fat foods and work out at least four to five days per week. But without a trainer to push her, her workouts grew shorter and less frequent. Four months later, her new clothes were hung in the back of her closet and she was pulling out size 14 jeans from the bottom drawer. It seemed like her cravings for sweets were stronger than before she'd lost the weight.

She was desperate to stop the rapid climb back into her former self. How could she waste all those hard months she'd invested getting healthy? Why wasn't the reward of actually *being* thin enough to motivate her to stay that way?

Lifestyle Failure Similarities

The vast majority of people who pay off consumer debt using home equity loans end up acquiring comparable or greater debt within two years. The same is true for people who follow any number of unsustainable diets. In fact, statistics reveal that about 95 percent of those who lose weight on a strict diet gain it back . . . and then some.

These two different scenarios have something important in common. Both illustrate that short-term solutions rarely produce lasting results. When we attempt to lose debt or weight by methods that are unsustainable, the results lack sustainability as well. For lasting success, we need to lose weight by the same method we plan to keep it off and we need to lose debt similarly. John, Sally, and Melissa needed to learn the power of the Sustainable Lifestyle Habit.

> Your lifestyle is the way you do things on a daily basis. It is a way of living that has become the norm in your life.

A *lifestyle* is a way of living that becomes the norm in your life. Whether it's health habits, work practices, money managing, or even raising your children, your lifestyle is the way you do things on a daily basis. If what you are doing is producing undesirable results, you need a new normal. A healthy and sustainable lifestyle is one that you can do most days for the rest of your life and still actually enjoy your life. You need to ask yourself a few questions to determine if your lifestyle plan is realistic and sustainable.

IF YOU WANT TO LOSE WEIGHT AND
KEEP IT OFF, ASK YOURSELF:

- Can I eat this way most days and not feel totally deprived?
- Can I lead a fairly normal life with this particular dietary approach?
- Will I be able to exercise and maintain this level of activity, or will I burn out?
- Do I have enough time to invest in this lifestyle most days for the rest of my life?

If the answer to those questions is no, you've probably just gone on another short-term diet or unrealistic exercise program. For example, if you decided to jump on the Dr. Atkins low-carb bandwagon, chances are you were thrilled when all the carb-like products hit the market that allowed you to eat something new. Unfortunately, these products proved that the diet just was not effective because of the chemistry of high-protein/low-carb effect. Once people added all the extra calories from the new designer products, most began to gain weight. Additionally, a diet that restricts carbohydrates diminishes your opportunity to nourish your body fully. I always wondered why God made the banana or apple if they are so bad for us. Did He forget to consult Dr. Atkins?

IF YOU WANT TO PAY OFF YOUR DEBT AND
STAY DEBT-FREE, ASK YOURSELF:

- Can I spend this way most days and not feel completely deprived?
- Can this kind of financial income and outgo be sustainable for the long term and still help me build the savings I need for a rainy day?
- Will I be able to live on this kind of a financial plan, or is it so restrictive that it sets me up to blow it and veer off the plan repeatedly?

- Am I willing to take the time necessary to sustain this spending plan in order to reach my financial goals?

A healthy and sustainable lifestyle is one that you can do most days for the rest of your life . . . and still actually enjoy your life.

The Power of Incremental Change

In his book *The Slight Edge*, Jeff Olson illustrates the power of incremental change in a vivid way. He writes,

> The water hyacinth is a beautiful, delicate plant that sports flowers ranging from a lovely purplish blue, to lavender and pink. You can find it floating on the surface of ponds in warm climates around the world. Although a single plant can produce as many as 5,000 seeds, the method it prefers for colonizing a new area is to grow by doubling itself, sending out short runner stems that become "daughter plants." On the first day of duplication, you probably won't even notice the hyacinth on the pond's surface. In fact, for the first few weeks you would have to search very hard to see any significant evidence of color. On day 15, the delicate flowers will cover about a single square foot of the pond's surface . . . a small dollop of color dotting the expanse of placid green. On the twentieth day, you may happen to notice a dense little patch of floating foliage, about the size of a small mattress. You could easily mistake it for an inflatable life raft, left behind during a family picnic. On day 29, one-half of the pond's surface will be open water. But, on the thirtieth day, the entire pond will be covered by a blanket of water hyacinth. You will not see any water at all![1]

SMALL STEPS

Incremental change and its compounding effect over time cannot be underestimated. It is a principle that can profoundly change your life if you pay attention to the small choices you make each day and intentionally add positive small steps that move you in the right direction. Most people who succeed in any area of life—from personal to professional or from relational to spiritual—do so because they understand this truth. People who fail simply give up too soon, often because they don't see fast enough results. Success and failure are rarely due to extraordinary skill or intelligence, but rather the willingness to take small steps each and every day.

Danna finally learned this in her own life after years of diet failure. She stopped chasing after fad diets and quick fixes that demanded an unrealistic lifestyle shift that was impossible to sustain. By making one or two healthier choices day after day and week after week, she began to reinforce her internal motivation and her belief that she could change her habits. Ellie and Bob made the same kind of small steps toward financial freedom to break out of what felt like crushing debt.

Don't allow your past failures to define your future success. Instead, take the small steps you can take today and watch them add up to a much brighter future. We will give you lots of practical ideas to do just that in future chapters.

> The things you do every day, the things that don't look like they matter, do matter. They not only make a difference—they make all the difference.
>
> —Jeff Olson

If you want to visit a beach in Oregon, using a map of California is not going to help you get there. To design a lifestyle that gets you where you want to go, you need to know what you really want—your ultimate goals. To reach those goals, you must design an action plan that will move you in the right direction. Following are the five steps that can make your goals attainable and allow you to live a productive and sustainable lifestyle.

Design Your Sustainable Lifestyle with Five Important Steps

Do you believe you are capable of reaching your life goals? If you don't, the teaching from the last chapter is essential for you to practice until you do because we always move in the direction of our deep-seated beliefs. Even though believing you can accomplish your goal is vital, belief without taking action is like getting in your car to go somewhere and never turning on the ignition and pulling out of the driveway.

My (Ellie's) son Philip's story is a great illustration of combining strong belief with key actions to meet even the most challenging of goals. No matter what you hope to achieve, you can take the same type of steps to realize your personal goals.

Philip was a big kid from the very beginning, weighing in at over nine pounds and measuring almost two feet tall. He was always goal oriented. From the time he could stack building blocks, he would try to get as many in place as possible before his older brother, Daniel, could knock them down. Determined, he would stack and Daniel would hack—over and over and over again. But a strange thing happened every time Philip hurried to build his blocks: he managed to stack up a couple more before his creation was toppled. This was a sign of things to come for this young man.

When Philip graduated from the Naval Academy and was selected to go to Stanford for his master's degree, he joined the triathlon team and wrote down his ultimate goal of running the Vineman Ironman Triathlon. This ultimate challenge begins with a 2.4-mile swim, followed by a 112-mile bike ride, and then is topped off by running a full marathon of 26.2 miles. Philip was in decent shape, but he had never completed the smallest of triathlons, much less attempted the granddaddy of all competitions. So he committed his goals to paper and took specific steps that helped him achieve this lofty goal. We hope his story and goal-setting technique will help you realize that you can reach your physical or fiscal goals by taking the same five steps.

STEP #1: DECIDE WHAT YOU WANT

Sometimes if we don't give our goals a specific date, then they are just dreams that may never become reality. We need to commit our goals to paper in order to solidify what we want. Whether your goal is to lose thirty pounds or wipe out thirty thousand dollars in debt, it's important to clarify your desires in writing. By deciding what you want, you will automatically begin to consider ways to get there. It's like choosing a destination for your family vacation. Knowing where you want to go makes all the difference in how you approach the trip. If it helps, write down your big goal first and then break it down into manageable, smaller parts.

Philip didn't decide to run an Ironman triathlon as his first race; he started with the shorter race called a sprint triathlon, which is a mere .47-mile swim, 12-mile bike ride, and 3.1-mile run. His first step was to join the Stanford triathlon team and sign up for his first race. He also decided that running the race solely to achieve a personal goal was a bit too myopic, so he added an incentive to the Ironman goal. He decided to raise money for the Semper Fi Fund, which is a nonprofit organization that benefits injured marines and sailors returning from combat. In addition, he decided to dedicate his run to two fallen marines, 1st Lt. Travis Manion and Maj. Douglas Zembiec. This further motivated him to work out with the team to reach his first goal on the path to a bigger and more noble goal of honoring heroes.

STEP #2: DECIDE WHERE TO START

They say the journey of a thousand miles begins with a single step, and when I (Ellie) chose to go skydiving a few years back and exited the plane at ten thousand feet, that first step was a doozy! You may feel like you are falling into the wild blue yonder unless you know who has your back. This step helps you to take action.

As we emphasized in Step #1, we don't decide to lose thirty pounds or thirty thousand dollars of debt as our first hurdle in reaching our goal. Instead, we break it down into smaller, more manageable steps. Your first step may be to start eating healthier with fewer calories consumed in the evening. Or you may set up a spending plan that identifies a few places to cut back on expenses and pay off debt. Taking a first step is the only way you will ever get to the finish line. Much like Ellie's skydiving instructor had her back on her first tandem jump, we have your back by giving you a gentle nudge toward this first big step. So take the dive and then move on to step three.

STEP #3: DECIDE WHAT DISTRACTS

When I (Danna) ventured into the area of health, people saw my presentations and my results and flocked to my side with opportunities to speak, endorse products, and fill my schedule with many good things. However, my professional and personal goals were not always best served by these opportunities. In fact, some of them were flat-out distractions.

When you begin to find success in reaching your goals, you may be faced with good things that can become distractions to the better thing—reaching your goal. Evaluate each opportunity in light of the written goals you have set for this area. Just as Philip had triathlon teammates, having a trusted friend or mentor may help you negotiate these distractions. A community of cheerleaders can be a valuable asset. Once you have a realistic strategy, if something knocks you off the path leading to your goal, then it is a distraction. But don't think that a distraction is the same thing as an obstacle, because it's not. The obstacle is, as the Wizard of Oz said, "A horse of a different color," and it is part of our next step.

STEP #4: DECIDE HOW TO OVERCOME OBSTACLES

There's a difference between a distraction and an obstacle. While the previous step, overcoming distractions, helps you filter out the non-essentials to your goal, this step helps you overcome the resistance that will surely block a path to your dream more fully than a 350-pound lineman blocks the running back from breaking through that line.

Both our youngest sons play football, and the team motto is "Do the Work." They even have T-shirts that remind them of their focus—to move the ball down the field and score a touchdown. The best way to over-come resistance is to focus on the goal line. Sometimes obstacles block our dreams, and we can't see the goal line. That's why having these steps committed to writing can make all the difference. You can see your goal in black and white, and that keeps you focused when the resistance comes.

If having teammates who share the same goal can help you overcome obstacles and focus, then partner with them for regular accountability. In some cases you may need to do something radical with those obsta-cles, such as cutting up a credit card or throwing out an uneaten pie. Develop a strategy that will help you do the work and decide ahead of time how you plan to overcome the obstacles that will surely come as you press on down the field.

STEP #5: DECIDE WHEN TO CELEBRATE

The first time Bob and I (Ellie) celebrated Philip's triathlon achieve-ments wasn't that sunny summer day in Sonoma Valley, California, when he completed his first Ironman. It was when he was racing in his first triathlon race. Bob and I positioned ourselves on the sprint course to cheer our son as he competed, and when he finished there was a cel-ebration with a team meal of chicken and waffles at the world-famous Roscoe's Restaurant. This final step is a way to celebrate your progress along the way toward your goal. Yes, you will eventually celebrate a final goal when you've lost those thirty pounds or thirty thousand dollars of debt, but it's also important to celebrate milestones along the way.

It also helps to surround yourself with a team of supportive fans who believe in you when you want to quit and who help you celebrate along the way. When Philip was racing in his Ironman, Bob and I found a halfway point on the course to set up our folding chairs and waited for a glimpse of our son. It was after the 2.4-mile swim and halfway through the 112-mile bike ride. I stood up and cheered each and every competitor riding by while Bob got the camera ready and sat down to read his news-paper until Philip's heat was due to arrive. When he appeared, I went crazy and shouted, "I love you, baby boy!" while Bob snapped photos.

This midpoint celebration was as important as the celebration at the end of the race because it kept him going.

When you reach your goal, be sure to take the time to thank those who have invested in your progress along the way. You may not celebrate by eating chicken and waffles, but your dream fulfilled will be all the more satisfying because of those people who helped you with the small steps on your way to your destination.

A Wealth of Financial Support

It's important to develop a support system in order to succeed. You can find "Money Buddy" at Crown.org or plug into a Financial Peace group found at www.DaveRamsey.com in order to find support and community. Many local churches have their own small groups. You can also choose to keep this simple and personal by teaming up with someone you know personally who deals wisely with his or her finances and is willing to mentor you in this area.

A Wealth of Physical Support

Experts agree that lasting lifestyle change is greatly enhanced when people develop a strong support system. It can be as simple as teaming up with your best friend and keeping each other accountable to exercise and eating goals. Or you can do something more structured, such as joining a program like Weight Watchers. I (Danna) have helped many women start small Scale Down support groups in their own homes so they can go through the program together. There are also lots of websites that provide virtual support, information, and opportunities to log your progress. I personally use a FitBit activity monitor and love the website support they offer at FitBit.com. I sync my FitBit each day and it records my activity directly onto my personal page where I can also compute my calories, set goals, and track my weight-loss progress. For me, it is an objective health buddy that doesn't ever give me false encouragement or praise—but it does celebrate my successes with visual reminders of the progress I have made!

Small Steps

As we've said, a journey of a thousand miles begins with a single step. But there is also the step that follows the first and the next one and so on and so forth. Every person can reach the goals in the way our previous section set forth by breaking down the bigger goal into smaller steps. Sometimes when you read a book like this one and get inspired to do these things, you don't take the time to do the work right away, and then the work gets stilted. Stephen Covey's groundbreaking book *The 7 Habits of Highly Effective People* had a profound effect on both of us in the way we viewed life.[2] He has a section that divides life events into four quadrants ranging from urgent and not urgent to important and not important. The four quadrants include those events that are:

1. Important and Urgent
2. Important and Not Urgent
3. Not Important and Urgent
4. Not Important and Not Urgent

One of the obstacles that gets in the way of reaching our goals is the tendency not to break our goals into smaller steps because we are primarily operating in the wrong quadrant, which is anything outside of quadrants one or two. Granted, when the boss asking for a report interrupts us, it's usually wise to respond even though it's not important, but it is urgent. However, the main emphasis in our lives would be best served by looking at those areas that are most important, such as our health and wealth.

LET'S REVIEW THE WAY TO REACH YOUR GOALS.

Step #1: Decide What You Want
Step #2: Decide Where to Start
Step #3: Decide What Distracts
Step #4: Decide How to Overcome Obstacles
Step #5: Decide When to Celebrate

We believe you can achieve your dreams by goal setting as we outlined above and also by breaking step two of those goals into smaller steps. Toward that end, we are going to encourage you to set goals in both of these critical areas by taking ten minutes to jot down your steps, breaking step two into smaller goals. To get you started, we've included Philip's worksheet and smaller steps that allowed him to complete the Ironman and raise seven thousand dollars for the Semper Fi Fund.

Step #1: Decide What You Want

- Run an Ironman
- Raise $7,000 for Semper Fi Fund
- Dedicate run to fallen marine heroes, 1st Lt. Travis Manion and Maj. Douglas Zembiec

Step #2: Decide Where to Start

- Join triathlon team in September 2011
- Follow daily workout/rest schedule for sprint distance for September through December
- Run two sprint triathlons (.47-mile swim, 12-mile bike ride, 3.1-mile run) from January 2012 to February 2012
- Follow daily workout/rest schedule for Olympic distance February through April 2012
- Run three Olympic triathlons (1-mile swim, 25-mile bike ride, 6.2-mile run) February through June 2012

- Follow daily workout/rest schedule for Half Ironman distance April through June 2012
- Run two Half Ironman Triathlons (1.2-mile swim, 56-mile bike, 13.1-mile run) April through June 2013
- Follow daily workout/rest schedule for Ironman June through July 2013
- Run one Ironman—July 2013

Step #3: Decide What Distracts

- Poor eating habits
- Mom's Oreo cookie balls
- Partying
- Additional duties that are important but not urgent
- Taking days off training for optional activities

Step #4: Decide How to Overcome Obstacles

- Get eating plan from triathlon coach
- Schedule meetings with coach and experienced triathletes
- Work out with team
- Take time to heal injuries
- Acquire race-worthy equipment
- Say no to optional expenses in order to afford to purchase equipment and to train
- Schedule workouts and map out courses ahead of time when traveling

Step #5: Decide When to Celebrate

- Each time after the longest distance accomplished on swim, bike, or run, whether in training or in a race
- After each race that I finish or beat my previous time
- When I see my parents at the finish line

The movie *The Rookie* (2002) tells the story of Texas high school baseball coach Jimmy Morris (played by Dennis Quaid), who makes the major leagues after agreeing to try out if his high school team made the playoffs. This movie emphasizes that it is not too late in life to follow your dreams. He gets his team in shape by beginning to throw some fast pitches in practice, which improves the players' hitting skills, and they win district. After they win, each of the players approaches their coach and says it's his turn. Coach Morris was scared spitless to make good on his word to his players and try out for the big leagues, but he did it anyway, and the rest is history. Watch this inspiring movie!

Applying the You Are What You Think Habit to the Top Ten Failure Factors

Earlier, we outlined the four fundamental habits that can help you transform your health and wealth. We also gave you a list of ten potential failure factors. Now let's take a brief look at each factor and how you can address the ones in your life by using the new habits in practical ways. Because the most foundational habit—You Are What You Think—is applicable to all the failure factors, we will first identify some potential lies that could be supporting these factors and replace them with truths you can apply through healthy self-talk. Then we'll comment on some other appropriate applications of other habits as well.

1. I SET UNREALISTIC GOALS.

Lie: I will be the same weight or size I was in high school. I will lose fifty pounds in two months. I will pay off debt I accumulated over five years in the next eighteen months. I will become a millionaire within two years.

Truth: I will lose weight, get healthier, pay off debt, and accumulate wealth by adopting new habits that are both healthy and sustainable. I care more about looking and feeling healthy than being an unrealistic size or weight. I care more about living within my means and being content than simply becoming rich.

2. I AM DRIVEN BY THE WRONG MOTIVES.

Lie: I need to be thin and/or rich to be loved and respected. I will be happy and fulfilled if I look my best and/or have financial freedom.

Truth: Being healthy and financially stable will enhance my life, but it will not define me. I desire to be wise and responsible so I can live a quality life and share my blessings with others.

3. I BELIEVE FAILURE IS INEVITABLE.

Lie: I have failed to keep weight off or get out of debt so many times that I know I will fail again. I never follow through or succeed in important ways.

Truth: I can be healthy and debt-free by taking small steps and making wise decisions each day. It may take me awhile, but I know if I don't give up, I will succeed.

4. I FULFILL THE NEED FOR IMMEDIATE GRATIFICATION TOO OFTEN.

Lie: I cannot say no to the things that bring me pleasure when I want them. I'm simply too weak. I lack willpower. I have a difficult life, and I deserve to indulge myself.

Truth: I choose to say no right now to some indulgences because I desire the greater benefit of being healthier and wealthier. I can see my bigger goal when I feel tempted, and that helps me make the right choice.

5. I AM INFLUENCED UNDULY BY OTHER PEOPLE.

Lie: The people in my life make it impossible for me to make wise choices and live a better lifestyle. People will think I'm poor if I'm always on a budget.

Truth: I am strong, and I take responsibility for my own choices. I don't care what other people think. No one can pressure me into doing something that holds me back from being my best.

6. I PRACTICE AN ALL-OR-NOTHING MENTALITY.

Lie: I can't start a new lifestyle until the first of the week, month, or year. I will never overeat or overspend again. I will pursue my new goal perfectly—or I won't do it at all.

Truth: I can start a new lifestyle right this moment and if I blow it, I will start fresh one minute from now. Each time I fall down, I get better at getting up. I am really good at learning to cut my losses and start over. Every little step in the right direction adds up!

7. I RATIONALIZE AND MAKE EXCUSES RATHER THAN TAKING RESPONSIBILITY.

Lie: It's not my fault that I've gained weight—it's my genes, my spouse's fault, my hormones, my body type, my dog's fault. I have bad money habits because I never had anything growing up. I can never get ahead because I can't make enough money at my job. I have so much debt (or excess weight) that it is impossible to ever turn things around.

Truth: I am gaining new knowledge and skills to change my habits. I realize that I will not be perfect, but I don't let that stop me from making midcourse corrections and starting fresh each day. I am motivated by each positive step I take, and I will not let occasional steps back stop me from pursuing my goals. Even though it may take a long while to reach my goals, I am confident I can if I take one day at a time and make better choices each day.

8. I HAVE DISPLACED EMOTIONAL ISSUES THROUGH OVERSPENDING AND OVEREATING.

Lie: When I am sad, tired, lonely, or frustrated, spending and/or eating makes me feel better. I have so little pleasure in life that I need to indulge myself with food or things so I am happy. Food is my best friend. Having nice things makes me feel important.

Truth: I am not defined by what I have or even who likes me. I have value as a human being, and I choose to deal with my emotional issues head-on rather than hide my difficulties or pain in unhealthy habits. I seek help to better understand how some of my actions are displaced emotions, and I work on new lifestyle habits that help me erase and replace the lies I believe.

9. I HAVE PROCRASTINATED RATHER THAN TAKING ACTION.

Lie: Tomorrow, next week, next month, next year . . . I will start to eat better, eat less, spend less, and save more. This is the last time I will overindulge, overspend, steal from my savings, avoid my workout, and make a big purchase without knowing all the facts.

Truth: Today is the day to make meaningful change. Right now is the right time to eat less, spend less, save more, eat healthier foods, and invest in myself. This very second, I am going to take action because now is the only moment I have control over.

10. I HAVE LACKED THE TOOLS TO MAKE COMPOUNDING INCREMENTAL CHANGE.

Lie: I don't know how to make a meaningful dent in my weight/ debt. What is the point in saving money if I have so many bills? What good is it to lose a few pounds when I need to lose fifty-plus? I don't know how to stay motivated. I cannot change.

Truth: Learning and practicing the four new lifestyle habits in this book and implementing a few practical tips each week will move me in the right health and wealth direction.

Applying the Other Habits to the Failure Factors

Here are some ideas of how you can use one of the other three habits to address any of the failure factors that may be a challenge in your life.

1. I SET UNREALISTIC GOALS.

As you set new goals, remind yourself that you want to adopt new behaviors that promote a sustainable lifestyle. Choose goals that support actions you can do most days for the rest of your life—and still enjoy your life. For example, create an eating plan that allows you to consume a reasonable volume of food you actually enjoy. Create a budget that gives you a bit of wiggle room to occasionally go out to eat or that has a reward incentive for staying on track for several months. Practice the 3D Habit by determining to review and adjust your goals on a regular basis. Remind yourself that the sacrifices you make today will be worth the future reward of a healthier body and/or bank account. Make sure your goals have ways you can accurately apply the In and Out Habit, which allows you to see the bottom line. This subject will be described more practically in chapter 6.

2. I AM DRIVEN BY THE WRONG MOTIVES.

Trying to meet someone else's expectations or reach outrageous goals diminishes your ability to create a sustainable lifestyle. Healthy motives influence those things that you have control over—your own thoughts and actions. Since you cannot control what others think or feel about you, stop dwelling on that which you cannot change. Healthy motives would include choosing to become lean and healthy so you can live a full life and enjoy the people you love. Changing your spending and saving habits so you can create greater security and less stress for your family is another healthy motive to energize your new lifestyle.

3. I BELIEVE FAILURE IS INEVITABLE.

Many people fail and believe failure is inevitable because they attempt drastic lifestyle changes that are difficult to maintain. By choosing one or two small lifestyle changes that are doable and succeeding at them, you can disprove the lie that failure is inevitable. Once you have mastered a few easy changes, add another perhaps more difficult challenge and give yourself permission to modify it to suit your life. Don't define your success by perfection. Instead, give yourself credit for every small step forward and realize that you don't ever really fail unless you give up completely!

4. I FULFILL THE NEED FOR IMMEDIATE GRATIFICATION TOO OFTEN.

Second only to changing your thoughts, the 3D Habit is a perfect antidote for this lifestyle-destroying failure factor. Become acutely aware of the situations where you are most tempted to cave in to immediate gratification rather than pursue your ultimate goals. Determine to design a new strategy *before* you encounter these scenarios. Avoid tempting situations as much as possible, but when you cannot, distract yourself from the temptation by choosing a new focus. Discover new ways to find fulfillment beyond overindulging. A positive approach is to clearly visualize yourself reaching your specific goals. Imagine in as much detail as you can what you will experience when you have accomplished your objective. Then ask yourself this question: "Is letting go of this now worth the benefit of what I will experience later?" If you cannot completely avoid a temptation (like a Thanksgiving meal or a desire to buy a new car when your current one is fine), then practice the delay technique by choosing not to have seconds for at least fifteen minutes or not making a final decision on the car without sleeping on it and asking yourself if you are making a wise long-term purchase.

5. I AM INFLUENCED UNDULY BY OTHER PEOPLE.

Living with someone who constantly tempts or cajoles you to make unhealthy financial and physical choices can be extremely challenging. In order for you to implement a positive and sustaining lifestyle, you must decide to do the right things for yourself while accepting the fact that the person or people you live with may not adopt your new habits. This certainly makes your journey more difficult, but not impossible. In your physical dimension, you need to realize that no one can make you eat food you choose not to eat or keep you from increasing your activity level. In your financial dimension, you have some bigger challenges if you are married to a person who will not partner with you to make some much-needed changes. It is important to remember that you can still control your part of the spending and saving. If necessary, meet with a trusted friend or counselor to explore ways to get your "spending spouse" on track. It's no wonder that a top reason for marital problems is finances! No matter how difficult your spouse may be, you can take control over your own actions. If just one person in a marriage decreases spending and makes wiser choices, it will benefit your bottom line.

6. I PRACTICE AN ALL-OR-NOTHING MENTALITY.

The small steps you take within your goals as described in the Sustainable Lifestyle Habit can help you move beyond your all-or-nothing mentality. By choosing to identify the distractions and obstacles in your way, you can overcome them more effectively. Use the 3D Habit as well and determine to remind yourself that every action you take counts—both the steps forward and the steps backward. Use the In and Out Habit philosophy to realize that just because you ate too much at lunch or spent too much at the mall, the expenditures (in calories or dollars) you make the rest of the day, week, or month still count.

7. I RATIONALIZE AND MAKE EXCUSES RATHER THAN TAKING RESPONSIBILITY.

Use the Sustainable Lifestyle Habit as a foundation for reinterpreting your lifestyle choices. It's been said that all excuses are equal—and they are equally worthless. No matter what excuses you used in the past, let them go and choose to focus and refocus daily on the goals you have set. Each time you are tempted to make an excuse, pull out a card with your top goals and current small-steps action plan and determine to distract yourself from the temptation to give up and make an intentional step in the right direction.

8. I HAVE DISPLACED EMOTIONAL ISSUES THROUGH OVERSPENDING AND OVEREATING.

It is common to seek sources of immediate gratification when we are experiencing negative emotions, such as anger, fear, frustration, boredom, or disappointment. One of the easiest ways to distract and indulge ourselves can be eating too much food or spending money carelessly. We all know the feeling of regret later when we reap the results of our poor choices. Practice the 3D Habit and determine ahead of time a more healthy response to your emotions. Delay immediate gratification— if only for ten minutes—exercising new self-discipline and self-talk. Distract yourself by engaging in an activity that does not produce a negative outcome—like calling a friend for support, taking a walk, or enjoying a warm soak in the tub.

9. I PROCRASTINATE RATHER THAN TAKING ACTION.

If we do nothing, we get nothing. This is the zero-sum game of the In and Out Habit played out in a life that constantly procrastinates. One of the simplest ways to make significant strides toward your goals is to do the most important hard stuff first each day. By addressing those things that require your greatest effort and concentration early, you set yourself up for success. Every night before you go to bed, choose the most important action item that will make the biggest impact in your journey toward your goal and do that one thing as early the next day as possible. Practice this new habit for twenty-one days, and you'll be amazed at the progress you have made.

10. I LACK THE TOOLS TO MAKE COMPOUNDING INCREMENTAL CHANGE.

No more excuses. You have an arsenal of tools at your disposal within the pages of this book. Sure, it will take time to evaluate and implement all the things you are learning. That doesn't mean you can't start taking some small steps immediately.

Practice the You Are What You Think Habit by identifying at least three lies you've been telling yourself and replace them with new self-talk messages. Write down those new messages. Now memorize those messages. Next, repeat the messages two to three times a day using something you do several times a day as a trigger.

Practice the Sustainable Lifestyle Habit by identifying your goals and a few initial small steps that will move you in that direction. Write this down and read it daily. Better yet—memorize it and include it in your healthy self-talk moments.

Practice the 3D Habit by recognizing common scenarios when you cave in to temptation to indulge and then determine a new way of responding. Delay immediate gratification as long as you can—step away from the fridge, step away from the store—and distract yourself with something different that you enjoy.

Practice the In and Out Habit by getting a reality check on your body and bank account. If you desire to lose weight, then learn exactly how many calories you are eating and burning. If you want to pay off debt and amass bigger savings, begin a realistic budget. (See chapter 6 for some practical ways to do both!)

If you found one or more appropriate ways to apply one of the four new lifestyle habits to any failure factors that challenge you, be sure to write down the new strategy in a notebook or on an index card so you can review it frequently to remind yourself to take a new approach.

Take Action

In the spaces provided below, write down your top four goals related to your health or wealth for the next year. For example:

1. Lose 40 pounds of fat from my body
2. Increase my energy
3. Pay off $20,000 in consumer debt
4. Begin a consistent savings plan

Write Down Your Goals

1. _____
2. _____
3. _____
4. _____

The goals you have written (assuming they are realistic and not something like "win a ten-million-dollar jackpot") are possible if you follow the strategy we've outlined and take small steps each day in the right direction.

Take Your Next Step

Now, choose just one health and wealth goal. Using the five steps detailed in this chapter, make some preliminary decisions in the following section for your top health and wealth goal. Later, you can write out a more detailed plan as you identify specific strategies shared in future chapters. If you visit our website at LeanBody-FatWallet.net, you can access a simple form for this purpose.

PART 2

Apply the Four Lean Body,
Fat Wallet Habits

6.

Balanced Bodies and Budgets

*Decrease debt and fat while increasing savings
and vitality by becoming a budget expert.*

Now that you understand the importance of developing the four Lean Body, Fat Wallet Habits and have learned new ways to address your emotional responses, it's time to notch up your efforts to burn down debt, burn off fat, and improve your physical and fiscal fitness. In this chapter, I (Danna) will take you through a few reality checks to help you eat less, burn more calories, increase your energy, and balance your energy equation for life. And I (Ellie) will provide simple charts and easy steps to develop a spending plan that is uniquely tailored to your individual and/or family's needs. From consumer debt to credit scores, I will show you how to balance your budget and diminish money stress once and for all.

Balancing Your Calorie Budget

A few years ago, I (Danna) realized I had slowly but surely gathered a little extra "energy storage" for the winter. I'd put on about ten pounds in the form of what I call "a menopause muffin top." It wasn't even noticeable to most people, but I knew it was there, and my size 6 jeans were stuffed high on a shelf in my closet and replaced by a more comfortable size 8. Now, size 8 is not by any means fat. But I felt better at my usual size and wondered if this was just a normal expectation of being a "mature" woman. After years of teaching and living the In and Out Habit, I decided to put my theory of losing fat to the test once again. I strapped on my favorite "virtual coach," a Caltrac activity monitor that told me exactly how many calories I burned all day long. I also went back to "calorie college," which meant calculating and inputting every morsel I ate into the Caltrac so that I knew from moment to moment whether I was burning more calories than I ate . . . or not. I knew that to burn off one pound of body fat, I needed to burn 3,500 calories more than I ate. To do this within the Sustainable Lifestyle Habit approach, I chose to net a positive 500 calories a day, which I calculated should result in a one-pound weight loss per week. The end result? Within six weeks, I was back in my size 6 jeans. Three months later, I was leaner and more toned than I was in my forties. Today at sixty, I'm in the best shape of my life.

That's how you balance a "body" budget! It's all about the numbers— even as you get older! Later in this chapter, I will share practical ways to decrease caloric intake and increase calorie burn so you can permanently balance your personal calorie budget. I'll also give my exciting triple-burn exercise tip that helped me reach my goal faster than ever.

WEALTH

> 66 Decrease debt while increasing savings
> by becoming a budget expert. 99

Couples have cited financial problems as a primary issue in the majority of divorces. Therefore, getting a grip on your family budget could be one of the best "divorce busters" you implement for the sake of your marriage and family. If you are single, you may want to get a "money buddy" to have someone to bounce budget issues off of and also to have accountability to stay within your spending plan. You and I are working on the In and Out Habit in a big way right now!

If you're married, I (Ellie) highly recommend you begin any budget discussion when both partners are relaxed. Breathe in, breathe out. Drink some warm milk. Have an Oreo. Have another one (don't tell Danna). Feeling relaxed now? No? Then try lighting an aromatherapy candle and put on some Frank Sinatra or Harry Connick Jr. mood music. Better? Good. Now take your serene mood right into the budgeting process with you.

You can create your own budget worksheet by writing out the following categories as noted on the basic spreadsheet below. The percentages and categories offered here are only guidelines that I have found are realistic and work for most people. For an online budget tool, go to EllieKay.com and check out the "Budget Percent Calculator."

CATEGORY	Current Income	Percentage of Current Income or Goal Budget	Current Spending or Current Budget	Current Status (Goal Budget Minus Current Spending)
Giving		10%		
Savings		10%		
Clothing/Dry Cleaning		5%		
Education/Misc.		5%		
Food		10%		
Housing/ Utilities/Taxes		30%		
Insurance		5%		
Medical/Dental		4%		
Recreation/ Vacation/Gifts/ Credit Card Debt		6%		
Transportation		15%		

Once you've created your own chart like the one above, take the following steps:

1. Fill in the first column with your current income.
2. Based on your current income, get the recommended percentages for the third column; this is your goal budget. This can be modified according to your current expenses. For example, if your spouse has a company car, then the goal budget may not be as much as 15 percent on transportation. If you are military and live on base, the housing expense may not quite be 30 percent. The goal budget is somewhat flexible, but the percentages are there as guidelines.
3. For the fourth column, figure out your current spending levels. This is the average you have spent for each category over the last six months. This tells you what you are currently spending and allows you the opportunity to compare your current spending levels with the recommended spending level percentages.
4. For the fifth and final column, take your current income and subtract what you are currently spending. This gives you your current spending status and indicates where you are spending over or under the recommended percentages in each category.
5. Once you see where you are on paper, then set up a new budget by cutting spending in one area (such as food or entertainment expenses) and increasing in another area (such as saving, tithing, or debt repayment).

Here is an example of one family's budget worksheet. The names have been changed, so don't call Tom or Sandy Wilson on the phone and tell them that you saw their budget in a book!

Sample Worksheet for the Tom and Sandy Wilson Family: $6,000/Monthly Income

CATEGORY	Current Income	Percentage of Current Income or Goal Budget	Current Spending or Current Budget	Current Status (Goal Budget Minus Current Spending)*
Giving	$600	10%	$250	$350
Savings	$600	10%	$400	$200
Clothing/Dry Cleaning	$300	5%	$450	($150)
Education/Misc.	$300	5%	$500	($200)
Food	$600	10%	$625	($25)
Housing/ Utilities/Taxes	$1800	30%	$1650	$150
Insurance	$300	5%	$275	$25
Medical/Dental	$240	4%	$200	$40
Recreation/ Vacation/Gifts/ Credit Card Debt	$360	6%	$650	($290)
Transportation	$900	15%	$985	($85)
Unaccounted for Spending			$200	($200)
Totals	$6000	100%	$6185	-$185 (new monthly debt)

*Numbers in parentheses are negative.

Evaluating the Wilsons

Crunching the numbers for your wallet is like stepping on the scale for your body. You find out exactly where you are and decide what new goals can be established to become more fiscally fit. The Wilsons thought they did just fine, but didn't realize that they were accruing more and more consumer debt every month. If you'll recall the overspending chart (from chapter 4) that details what spending one hundred dollars a month in credit will cost in the long run, you can see how the Wilsons were getting themselves in pretty bad shape through adding just a little more debt each month.

There were obvious areas where the Wilsons weren't giving or saving close to what they could be in their situation. They also saw that there was money they couldn't account for each month. This is money that was spent when they were out and about and just seemed to evaporate from their account. Here is what the Wilsons decided to do after they crunched the numbers:

1. Take the money they were under spending in a category and move it to a category where they were overspending (e.g., from housing to credit card debt).
2. Track their family spending better to account for the unexplained "loss" of $200 per month.
3. Take the "lost" money ($200) and put it toward either saving or giving.
4. Cut the fat in categories where they were overspending (e.g., carpool to work twice a week to save on gas money and use coupon-saving strategies to reduce food expenses).
5. Establish a new budget based on percentages and the goals they wanted to achieve (such as tithe and save more, get rid of credit card debt, and get the same goods by learning ways to save money).

Another Budgeting Option from Danna's Desk

Despite the fact that I (Danna) spent eight years as a financial expert in the retirement division of a Fortune 100 Company and was the marketing manager responsible for all the sales staff and accounts in northern California and Nevada, I readily admit that I pretty much hate numbers. I learned some important principles about money in those corporate years and realized no matter how much I hated those pesky digits, I needed to find a palatable way to keep my financial budget as well balanced as my body budget.

In recent years, I manage several budgets including my speaking and outreach ministry (Women of Purpose), my household, as well as my family mountain cabin that is an active rental property. Understanding some of Ellie's essential budgeting techniques, I created a simple Excel budget spreadsheet and have used it consistently for over eight years. While my categories don't indicate the specific percentages that Ellie encourages people to strive toward, I have implemented them into my overall budgeting plan with a special priority on giving and saving the first tenth of our income.

The Smiths' fabricated spreadsheet that follows is similar to the one my husband, Lew, and I use for our household income. It uses simple Excel programming to total columns and allow for easy calculations.

Sample Budget

Monthly Bills	Amount	Comments	Income	Amount
Charitable Giving	$500	*Church and World Vision*		
Savings	$500		Bank Balance	$500
House Payment/Rent	$1,200		His Income	$3,000
Life Insurance	$100		Her Income	$2,000
Health Insurance	$150		Other Income	
Car Insurance	$200			
Car Payment(s)	$350			

Monthly Bills	Amount	Comments	Income	Amount
Gasoline/Car Maintenance	$350			
Utilities (Water)	$100			
Utilities (Gas)	$50			
Utilities (Electric)	$150			
Phone/Cable/ Internet	$150			
Cell Phone Service	$200			
Credit Card #1	$100			
Credit Card #2	$100	*Paid off this month!*		
Credit Card #3				
Personal Care (Hair-cuts, etc.)	$150			
Food and Household Supplies	$500			
Discretionary	$200		**Total Income**	**$5,500**
Unexpected Expenses			**Less Expenses**	**$5,050**
Total	**$5,050**		**Balance**	**$500**

A Few Pointers

After years of using this type of budget, I (Danna) find that making weekly adjustments as I pay bills or grocery shop helps keep me on track. For example if my water bill turns out to be fifty dollars more than anticipated, I change the amount and make a decision where to adjust my budget. Unexpected expenses almost always must come from my discretionary spending, as

I don't want to tap into our savings. We are committed to giving faithfully to our church and sponsoring children through World Vision, so those stay a high priority. If another bill turns out to be less than expected (which rarely happens), then we have a little more wiggle room.

You will also see that at the top of the income column, I keep an entry of my current bank balance. I check that a few times a week when I am paying my bills online and make sure that no unexpected charges show up. This budget reality check usually takes me less than ten minutes and helps me make wise decisions all week long! For help setting up your own spreadsheet budget, visit our website at LeanBody-FatWallet.net.

Stay on the Same Sheet of Music

Families usually have favorite restaurants, movies, and even special songs that reflect the character and tastes of the family. Your budget will be just as unique as your family. It will be based on variable factors, such as your family's size, geographical location, debt load, and income.

When Bob and I (Ellie) first set up a budget, we realized that both of us wanted to have healthy finances, even though we approached money differently. As you go through the sometimes painful process of establishing and sticking to a family budget, it is important to make a real commitment to these important issues. We also realized that we didn't need to go overboard by pinching our pennies so tightly that it strained our relationship and took all the enjoyment out of life. So we allowed for an occasional indulgence, implemented budget-cutting techniques slowly, and modified our plan as needed. As time went on, we fine-tuned some aspects of our budget and then did an annual checkup to make adjustments that allowed the budget to become a part of our Sustainable Lifestyle Habit.

Use the 3D Habit for Common Budget Busters

There are a few problem areas that can throw a budget off course in a matter of seconds, sending it reeling toward disaster. This is where implementing the 3D Habit (determine, delay, and distract) can greatly help you to stay on track. Here are a few tips to avoid these pitfalls.

DEBT OR CREDIT

You may choose to adopt a cash-only policy when it comes to your budget, setting up an envelope system where you place the budgeted amount of cash in envelopes marked "food," "entertainment," "gas," and so on. When the money runs out, you stop spending until the end of the allotted period (generally one to two weeks, depending upon how you are paid). A regular peek at the amount of cash left in each envelope is a vivid reminder of your budget commitment. If credit has become a habit, then you might even do something drastic, like cut up your credit cards.

IMPULSE BUYING

Nothing busts a budget like impulse buying. If this is an area where you struggle, it's important to be proactive and address the issue *before* you take action. If you don't drive to the mall and go to your favorite department store, you won't be as likely to spend unbudgeted money. *Determine* to practice the habits you've been learning every day so you will have the internal motivation needed the next time you are tempted. Practice the You Are What You Think Habit by giving yourself new self-talk messages until they become your dominant thoughts. Follow the In and Out Habit by reviewing your budget frequently and giving yourself a reality check that is a reminder of your bottom line. Implement the 3D Habit by determining in advance what you have budgeted and how you will delay any unplanned purchases or distract yourself from caving in to impulse buying. For example, if you're an online buyer, overspending on the Internet, submit to being accountable to a roommate or spouse who will check your browser for daily activity. If you live alone . . . pull the plug!

A good way to short-circuit impulse buying of unbudgeted items is to follow the thirty-day rule, which in essence is the *delay* portion of the 3D Habit. If it's not in your budget, delay the purchase for thirty days. During that month, find two other items that are similar and compare prices. If it's still available at a good price, and it fits the next month's budget, then buy it. You will likely find that you're buying less stuff because this delay gives you the opportunity to get beyond the impulse.

COMFORT SPENDING

Many couples indulge in comfort spending on clothes, sports equipment, expensive restaurants, and excessive entertainment, to name a few. This unhealthy habit of throwing caution to the wind just to live in the "now" is a budget buster that will keep you living in debt. However, most of us do not reform our unhealthy habits overnight. At the very least, begin to modify and become more intentional about these comfort indulgences. Even cutting back on *some* of this kind of spending can add up positively. For example, if you can't afford to go out to eat four times a month, then go only twice. If you feel you cannot live without some occasional "retail therapy," then avoid major department stores and go to a discount store with a set budget in mind. It's amazing how much you can buy for forty dollars or less if you shop wisely.

GIFTS

Think about the gifts you buy for relatives, teachers, baby showers, weddings, birthdays, Valentine's Day, Mother's Day, Father's Day, kids' birthdays, and anniversaries. This doesn't even cover the biggie: Christmas. The first thing we should do is evaluate the "why" of gift-giving. Do we really have to give a material gift in each circumstance? Wouldn't a card work just as well in some cases? What about baked goods or homemade gifts found on Pinterest.com instead?

Occasionally, giving a gift may put the receiver under a sense of obligation. Think through each of these gifts to put them into perspective and manage your budget at the same time. And though "It's the thought that counts" may sound like a worn-out cliché, it can be a worthy sentiment if a modest gift is given with an authentic expression of feeling toward the recipient.

VACATIONS

An extravagant vacation on a tropical island or a romantic getaway to Europe may seem like a dream. But it can turn into a nightmare for a budget when you get the credit card statement. The joy of a week away is often long forgotten while the monthly stress of the remaining debt may linger for more than a year. Some advance planning can salvage the concept of a dream vacation while keeping it from becoming another budget buster. Too often, people fail to consider more than the big costs of travel and accommodations. But everything adds up . . . and quickly. Count the cost and consider vacations that can give you the fun, opportunity, and relaxation you desire without the lingering debt. Even when you have plenty of savings to spend on vacations, ask yourself if there's a less expensive way to do the same things. If there is, then plan it into your budget and enjoy every cent spent. I'll give more tips on how to plan a vacation on a budget in chapter 9.

HEALTH

66 Decrease fat while increasing vitality by
becoming a body budget expert. **99**

In a perfect world, we would crave only healthy food, eat only when we were hungry, and move all day long. Since that doesn't seem to come naturally to many of us, we have to make conscious choices to balance our imperfect lifestyles and habits.

Calories In Versus Calories Out

The body is a calorie-burning and -storing machine. We make deposits into our calorie bank account every day in the form of food and drink. We also make withdrawals in the form of energy or calories burned. Unlike our financial bank account, most of us would prefer to be a little overdrawn in the calorie department, burning more calories than we eat, at least until we use up all of our excess fat accounts. There are two main times when our bodies will use already stored fat for fuel—when we burn more calories than we eat and when we are moving aerobically.

Years ago, when I (Danna) realized that the bottom line to fat management was calories in versus calories out, losing weight finally made sense to me. I felt as if I were freed up to eat the way I wanted, without so many diet rules. I knew that eating healthy food was important, but focusing on total calories gave me more freedom to make lifestyle changes that I could realistically work into my day-to-day life.

The advantage of understanding how your body uses calories is that it gives you complete freedom to design your preferred eating plan based on your personal likes and dislikes. It gives flexibility to make midcourse corrections each day or week. I'll show you several simple ways to decrease your calories consumed so you can lose weight without ever going on another diet. Before I do, there's some important information you need to know about your metabolism so you can proceed safely.

Resting Metabolic Rate (RMR)

To reach *and* sustain your weight-loss goals, it is helpful to understand how you burn fat. Genetics, health, and diet history influence your ability to access fat stores effectively. If you become too enthusiastic about losing weight too quickly and eat too little or exercise too much, you may find that your weight-loss progress is stalled.

Most people are aware that prolonged low-calorie dieting can slow down one's metabolism. Newer studies reveal that some people, especially women, can slow their metabolism by experiencing a net deficit as little as five hundred calories each day. Your RMR (resting metabolic rate) is the number of calories you burn in twenty-four hours doing absolutely nothing. One way to ensure that you maintain a healthy metabolism is never to eat less than your personal RMR. (See the following explanation and charts to guesstimate your RMR.)

Your RMR is influenced by age, weight, height, sex, and lean muscle mass (or body fat percentage). As you age, it naturally decreases due to the fact that you lose muscle mass, which is often described as the engine of your body, causing you to burn fewer overall calories. However, a regular routine of cardiovascular exercise and strength training can sustain a healthy metabolism at any age.

To calculate a *rough* guesstimate of your RMR, multiply your current weight times 10 for females and 11 for males. For example, if you are a woman weighing 140 pounds, your RMR would be 1,400.[1] Understand that if you are quite overweight, your RMR is still related to your current weight because your body is designed to naturally support all its living cells no matter how much excess fat you may carry. As you lose body fat, your RMR will drop—not because your metabolism is damaged, but because there is less of you to support. If you are more than fifty pounds overweight, I recommend you consult your doctor or a health coach to help you determine a realistic RMR to calculate your minimum calorie intake. An excellent website to find several health and wellness calculators including an RMR calculator is Health.Discovery.com.

The tables below will help you get a general idea of how different factors can impact your personal numbers. For example, a female who is five foot seven and weighs 140 pounds will experience a decrease in her RMR as she ages, as expressed in the following chart:

Age	RMR	Decrease Total
20	1477	
30	1430	(47)
40	1383	(94)
50	1336	(141)
60	1289	(188)
70	1242	(235)

In the second example, a female who is five foot seven and forty years old will have the following RMR dependent upon her weight:

Weight	RMR
140	1383
150	1426
160	1470
170	1513
180	1557
190	1600
200	1644

Three Steps to Promote Fat Burning

You can enhance your metabolism and promote fat burning by consistently taking three key steps:

STEP #1: NEVER EAT LESS THAN YOUR RMR

Support your RMR by never starving yourself, and also avoid burning more than five hundred to six hundred calories more than you eat unless you are working with a professional who can help ensure you are not damaging your metabolism. Remember that your objective is to maintain a sustainable lifestyle, which means losing weight the same way you plan to keep it off. By losing about one pound a week, you will be much more likely to keep it off.

STEP #2: SUPPORT A HEALTHY METABOLISM
BY DOING MUSCLE WORK REGULARLY

One pound of fat only burns about five calories per day, but a pound of muscle, which takes up less space than its fat counterpart, burns about fifty calories per day. If you were to increase your overall muscle mass by two pounds in the next year, you would consistently burn an extra one hundred calories per day, which in turn would promote a ten-pound weight loss if the intake of calories did not increase. To increase muscle, add weight lifting and toning exercises four to five times per week to your exercise routine. I choose to include about fifteen minutes of light weights, leg lifts with leg weights, abdominal exercises, and squats to my daily routine. You don't have to join a gym or hire a trainer to keep your muscles toned. In fact, you can incorporate your own body weight into many exercises and never pick up a weight.

STEP #3: SUPPORT A HEALTHY METABOLISM
WITH FREQUENT AEROBIC EXERCISE

Our bodies burn fat best during aerobic (sustained, big muscle) exercise like walking, running, swimming, biking, and so on. Because most of our lifestyles are sedentary, we must intentionally add movement into our lives. Even if you are standing most of the day, you are not burning very many calories. To maximize metabolism and calorie burn, you need to make daily aerobic exercise as important as daily meals! In another chapter I'll share why the most aerobically fit people often live longer and look younger than their sedentary counterparts. If you dislike exercise or believe you don't have time to squeeze it into your busy life, I encourage you to change your thinking and determine to make it a priority if you want to get and stay lean for life.

The In and Out Habit in Action

To develop a sustainable lifestyle and maintain a balanced approach to weight loss, it is important to work on both sides of the energy equation. Most people who want to lose weight focus primarily on changing the intake side and end up failing. As I've already noted, burning calories is equally and sometimes even more important.

FAT-BURNING FACTS

The average woman burns about 1,700 calories per day. I know that may sound high to some of you, but it's not high at all. In centuries past, most people burned at least 25 percent more calories. Think about how they lived. There were no power vacuums or automatic washers, no drive-through restaurants or dry cleaners. People walked everywhere and engaged in physical labor every day. Today, for many of us, the extent of our exercise includes getting into the shower and walking to our cars. We drive to covered parking, take elevators to our offices, roll around on wheeled chairs, and e-mail our business associates.

ONE POUND EQUALS 3,500 CALORIES

There are 3,500 calories in one pound of fat. Take a moment to visualize one pound of fat by remembering what a pound of raw hamburger looks like. It's really quite sizeable. If you eat enough calories and actively burn 500 calories more than you eat each day, you will burn off about one pound of fat every week. That could be 52 pounds in one year. You don't have to change your life dramatically.

For every 100 extra calories burned per day, you can lose about one pound of fat per month. For a 140-pound woman, that is the equivalent of walking about .8 miles. Two hundred extra calories equals approximately 20 pounds in one year; 400 equals 40; 500 equals 50, and so forth. Of course, this is assuming your caloric intake does not go up. Sounds simple, doesn't it? It is. Your greatest obstacle is building the habits that result in consistent action steps that add up to reaching your goal one calorie at a time.

A SIMPLE CALORIE BUDGET TO BURN OFF
ONE POUND OF FAT PER WEEK

While we won't address nutrition in fine detail in this book, it is ideal not only to decrease the amount of food you eat but also to notch up the quality. You don't need a PhD in nutrition to know that eating more fruits, vegetables, and lean proteins while eating fewer processed, empty calories is great for your overall health.

No matter what type of foods you choose to eat, you can follow a simple calorie budget and lose one pound per week until you reach your ultimate goal by burning 500 calories more than you eat on average each day. Unless you are already very active and engage in at least 30 minutes of aerobic activity most days, I recommend working both sides of your energy equation to reach your goal.

BURN 250 CALORIES MORE / EAT 250 CALORIES LESS

Simply burn about 250 calories more and eat 250 calories less than you normally do each day to create a net "positive burn" of 500 calories per day. That adds up to 3,500 calories, which equals one pound of body fat. Don't become impatient. It took a long time to put on excess pounds and it takes even longer to burn them off. But by taking it slow and taking small steps you can sustain, you will not only lose the fat but you will keep it off.

A LITTLE ONLINE ASSISTANCE

Two free websites that include calorie/food counts, activity trackers, and goal setting that I like and find user friendly are: ACalorieCounter .com and SparkPeople.com. SparkPeople also has lifestyle apps available for your smartphone.

There are many simple ways to increase calorie expenditure and decrease calorie intake. The key is to choose strategies that work best to support your goal of designing your own Sustainable Lifestyle Habit. I will share my favorite fat-burning and calorie-saving tips next. Consider which ones would work best with your new lifestyle.

First, take a look at the following chart to see how you can average a one-pound weekly fat loss. This is a one-week example of a person who is trying to eat about 250 to 300 calories less than usual per day and burn at least 250 calories more. I highly recommend using an activity monitor such as a Caltrac or a Fitbit to accurately track calorie burn all day long. In this example, the person had a net (excess) burn of calories that ranged from 300 to 800 calories per day for a total excess burn of 3,500 calories by the end of the week. This demonstrates how to adjust your eating and activity based on the demands of your life, which can vary day to day, and still reach your goals.

Day	Calories In	Total Calories Burned	Activity Calories	Net Calories
1	1600	2100	700	500
2	1500	2200	800	700
3	1700	2100	700	400
4	1600	1900	500	300
5	1400	2200	800	800
6	1600	1900	500	300
7	1400	1900	500	500
Totals	10,800	14,300	4,500	3,500

After decades of lifestyle coaching, I can almost hear some of you yelling into your books, "I will *never* count calories; it's too much work!" Perhaps not—but *never* say *never*! In my personal experience, those people willing to take an accurate look at their bottom line (calories eaten versus calories burned) on a daily basis, have not only lost weight but also kept it off permanently. There is something very powerful about a constant reality check. It works for both your body and your bank account. Nevertheless, I will give you several ideas for cutting calories—even those that won't require you to specifically count them. But beware: most people are really great at denial and rationalization when they don't have the facts staring them in the face. If you aren't making good progress within a few weeks with the first three tips, move to Strategy #4, and I promise I won't say, "I told you so."

Danna's Five Best Strategies for Consuming Fewer Calories

STRATEGY #1: PORTION CONTROL

One of the simplest ways to cut calories is to practice portion control. Many weight-loss companies that offer prepackaged foods are making a fortune doing something you can easily do for yourself. Unfortunately, our culture no longer knows what normal food portions look like. We are so accustomed to food being supersized that we think we are being cheated when average portions are served. After living in Europe for two years, I realized how outrageous the American diet has become. It's no wonder that more than half our population is overweight.

You can practice healthy portion control with these three simple steps:

1. Never reduce or cut down on vegetables, and rarely cut back on fruit unless you are eating excessive amounts of high-fat or high-glycemic foods like avocados, bananas, and apples. One each per day of those higher-calorie, higher-carbohydrate foods is enough. I include foods such as corn and potatoes in this starch category.
2. Consider what has been a "normal" portion for you in the past and reduce it by at least 25 percent. If you've been consuming an average of two thousand calories per day, you just reduced your intake by about five hundred calories. Simple, yes?
3. Be honest about the empty calories you consume. Desserts and other sweets fall into this category as well as chips, crackers, and even bread. Try to cut these types of food in half.

What is so great about this approach is that you don't have to give up anything you love. You simply eat less of it. Now, that should not be an excuse for not giving your body more quality, nutrient-dense foods. But it does allow you to scale down the calories you are consuming slowly and scale up the quality in a way that works for you.

STRATEGY #2: EAT 30 TO 50 PERCENT LESS THE LAST FOUR HOURS OF YOUR DAY

Most people eat most of their calories in the last four to six hours of their day—just hours before they go to bed. That is the absolute worst time as it is almost impossible to burn off those calories unless you exercise in the evening as well. It has been proven that we metabolize our calories much more efficiently if we eat four to five smaller meals all day long rather than two or three larger ones. However, we also need to design a lifestyle that we can enjoy and sustain. Couple that with the fact that the family dinner is one of the best bonding experiences known to man, and we have a real dilemma.

Whether you cook and feed a family every night or eat alone, you can simply choose to eat 30 to 50 percent less food the last four hours of your day. I do this by serving my meal on a salad plate, choosing not to eat bread with dinner, and indulging in my *predetermined* fun foods in the middle of the day rather than after dinner. Sometimes I simply practice portion control as described above, and sometimes I count my calories and choose to eat what most appeals to me based on a predetermined (there's that word again) number of calories I know is reasonable. This allows me to participate in family meals while maintaining a lean body. When I go out to eat, I often talk my husband or a girlfriend into sharing a meal with me (Ellie loves this money-saving idea), and we benefit physically and financially.

STRATEGY #3: FUEL AND BURN ALL DAY LONG

Imagine that your body is like a car with a five-gallon gas tank. This would require you to pop into a gas station much more frequently to refuel since your storage capacity is so limited. I would *hate* having a car like that. However, your body burns calories much more efficiently when you fuel and burn all day long rather than consume two or three large meals.

Your body actually "knows" about how many calories it needs at specific times of day based on your current habits. If you eat more than you will likely burn, it becomes highly efficient at storing those excess calories as fat. But if you eat frequent yet smaller meals and snacks, your body can burn them quickly. So whether you are eating 1,400, 1,800, 2,200, or more calories per day—eating them in five to six smaller meals/snacks will result in a better burn-off rate. This is especially true for postmenopausal women, who find it easier to put on weight and harder to take it off. In my own experience, this strategy has helped me not only avoid gaining the average six pounds a year many post-menopausal women realize, but also actually maintain a lower body weight and fat percentage than I maintained in my forties.

STRATEGY #4: CUT OUT ALL PROCESSED FOODS, WHITE FLOUR, AND SUGAR

This simple strategy is a very healthy way to eliminate almost all the empty calories from your diet—foods none of us need and where most of us consume the extra calories that cause weight gain. The challenge with this approach is that you alone can decide if you can sustain this stricter lifestyle and maintain it indefinitely. Most people who adopt this approach do so for more than simply weight loss, but for the health and longevity benefits as well. It can be very effective; however, those who "fall off the wagon" and back into the bag of chips or cookies often fall hard. If you are not ready to take the plunge (and in full disclosure—I have never completely eliminated "fun food" from my diet)—a modified version of this strategy can become a helpful add-on to one of the other options. For example, you may decide to allow yourself processed foods only once or twice a week on predetermined days and in predetermined amounts. One habit I chose to implement years ago and rarely stray from is that I never eat any empty calories before lunch, such as white bagels, pancakes, doughnuts, and so on. My exception may be Christmas morning when we have my famous whole-wheat banana bread, which while pretty healthy, contains sugar.

STRATEGY #5: THE ULTIMATE STRATEGY: GO TO "CALORIE COLLEGE"

As I've already said, counting calories is the most accurate way to get a reality check on exactly how much you are eating. It will give the information you need to determine food choices. If you are truly serious about getting lean, I encourage you to go to "calorie college" and learn what you are really burning for at least twenty-one days. Keep a log during that time, and record the information shared in the earlier chart. I know for some, this sounds like awful drudgery. However, few of us would consider going through a whole month without checking our bank balance because it could easily become overdrawn. But that's what we do many days with our calorie accounts. If calories are the bottom line, it makes sense to know what the bottom line really is. If you can get through forty days of counting, you will be amazed at how rarely you need to look up caloric content. And even if you stop actively counting on a daily basis, you will be amazed at how the information you learned sticks with you and gives a more accurate conception of what you are really eating. What at first may seem tedious will eventually become a lasting tool that keeps you on track.

Danna's Six Best Strategies for Burning More Calories

Eating less each day only addresses one side of your "energy" budget. Burning more calories allows you to eat a reasonable amount of food, improve your fitness, and reduce excess fat stores effectively. Consider the following strategies to become a fat-burning machine!

STRATEGY #1: DO THE EXERCISE AND ACTIVITIES YOU LIKE BEST

People often ask me, What is the best exercise to lose weight and keep it off?

My answer: The exercise or activity you will do consistently. *("None" is not an acceptable option!)*

STRATEGY #2: EXERCISE AT THE TIME OF DAY THAT WORKS BEST FOR YOU

People also ask me, What is the best time of day to work out?

My answer: The time *you* will work out most consistently.

My point is obvious: finding an activity you enjoy and a time that works best for you will ensure consistency—which is far more important than getting a maxed-out, high-calorie-burning, intense workout that you hate and only do occasionally!

All that being said, it is essential to find a form of aerobic exercise that you enjoy since that type of exercise burns fat most effectively. Whether that activity is swimming, walking, running, engaging in group exercise, or following along to a video in the living room—it does not matter. If you need lots of variety or prefer exercising outdoors, then design exercise to meet those preferences. By making these kinds of choices that work best for your life, you are building the Sustainable Lifestyle Habit into your exercise regimen. Go back to chapter 5 and the section on goal setting, and create a plan for reaching a specific activity or fitness goal for the next three, six, or even twelve months. Be realistic. If you've been a couch potato for the last few years, don't plan to run a marathon in the next three months! Do challenge yourself, though. You will be amazed at how much your body can and will change by slowly but surely increasing activity—and don't quit!

STRATEGY #3: INCLUDE HEALTHY SELF-TALK TO OVERCOME A "COUCH POTATO" MIND-SET

If you find yourself dreading even a favorite type of workout, you may need to pay special attention to the You Are What You Think Habit and repeat several important self-talk messages throughout the day. Here are a few statements you can use or modify:

- *I crave exercise. I look forward to my daily workouts.*

- *I love the way my body feels after a good workout, and that motivates me to keep going.*
- *I know my body is changing one cell at a time and getting stronger every day I stay active.*
- *I am an active person who loves being strong and fit, and my lifestyle proves it.*

Perhaps for some of you, these statements sound like outright lies. Don't despair. If you tell yourself these messages and move your body regularly, you will not only come to believe them but also reap some great physical rewards!

STRATEGY #4: CONSIDER DAILY EXERCISE YOUR ULTIMATE GOAL

You may have noticed the first self-talk sentence above includes the words "daily workouts." This may seem extreme, but in our very sedentary culture, most of us need to find ways to move our bodies intentionally each and every day. That does not mean that you need to take the *Biggest Loser* approach and spend three to four hours in the gym or with a personal trainer every day. But it does mean that you at least take a thirty-minute stroll after dinner or park your car at the end of the parking lot when shopping. One of the things I choose to do when I am spending a lot of time at my computer (like writing this book) is to use my downstairs bathroom rather than the one right across from my office upstairs. While I'm up, I will sometimes jump on my treadmill for a five- to ten-minute break just to get the kinks out. Even though I don't burn massive calories, the benefit adds up after a four-hour writing session with an hourly break. It also increases the blood flow to my brain and improves my creativity.

STRATEGY #5: USE AN ACCURATE ACTIVITY MONITOR AS MOTIVATION TO MOVE MORE

One of the best weight-loss tools I've ever used is a Caltrac activity monitor. Clipped on to your waistband, it can determine within 1- to

3 percent accuracy how many calories you are burning all day long in a wide variety of activities. It also assesses your RMR and allows you to manually input the calories you eat. Another great device is a Fitbit monitor. Both are excellent activity monitors that can give an accurate assessment of how many calories you are really burning and motivate you to move more all day long. I highly recommend using one to help you lose unwanted fat and maintain that loss.

STRATEGY #6: FIND CREATIVE WAYS TO GET LONGER, HIGHER-BURNING AEROBIC WORKOUTS

Once exercise becomes a regular part of your daily routine and you are noticing the benefits, start to slowly notch up the frequency, intensity, and duration of your workouts for increased fat-burning potential. I've included a chart below that shows which activities burn more calories. If you burn an extra one hundred calories per day by adding about ten minutes to your daily aerobic routine, that will add up to a ten-pound weight loss in one year. And once you reach your goal, that means one hundred "free" calories you could consume each day simply because you are active!

Danna's Triple-Burn Exercise Tip

After many years of teaching high-impact aerobic classes, my lower back cannot take the pounding it once did—so running or other high-impact activities that allow me to burn calories quickly are out of the question. Nevertheless, I discovered a safe way to triple my calorie burn—by walking on a treadmill at a 12 percent grade. By walking one mile on a flat surface, I normally burn about 125 calories, but at 12 percent, I burn a whopping 375 calories! That's three times as much fat burned!

When I set my goal to lose my "menopause muffin," I determined to work out at least six days per week for at least thirty minutes and to burn an average of 700 to 1,000 activity calories each day. That made the "intake" side of my energy equation (eating) pretty easy to deal with. My

RMR at age sixty is about 1,250 calories per day. With my extra activity calories, I averaged about 2,200 calories burned each day. To lose one pound per week, all I needed to do was eat about 1,700 calories each day to burn off one pound per week. (Note: 500 net calories times 7 days equals 3,500 calories, or one pound of fat!)

Calorie Burn Chart

ACTIVTY	15 Min.	30 Min.	45 Min.	60 Min.
Aerobics (high-impact)	104	207	311	414
Aerobics (low-impact)	74	148	222	296
Bicycling (12 to 14 mph)	118	236	354	472
Box aerobics	133	265	398	530
Circuit weight training	118	236	354	472
Downhill skiing	74	148	222	296
Golf (carrying clubs)	81	162	243	324
In-line skating	104	207	311	414
Jumping rope (moderate)	148	295	443	590
Kayaking	74	148	222	296
Racquetball	104	207	311	414
Rowing machine	150	300	450	600
Running (8.5-minute mile)	170	339	509	678
Stair climber	105	210	315	420
Stationary biking (vigorous)	155	310	465	620
Step aerobics	169	337	506	674
Tennis (singles)	118	236	354	472
Walking (12-minute mile, flat)	113	225	413	550
Walking (15-minute mile, flat)	88	175	263	350
Walking (Treadmill, 15-minute mile, 12% grade)	264	528	792	1056
Water aerobics	59	118	177	236
Weight lifting (vigorous)	89	177	266	354
Yoga	59	118	177	236

*Based on a 130-pound woman

7.

Fat Cells and Fat Sales

*Learn to manage unintentional consumption
by using these helpful tips.*

If you've wondered why you can't stick to a new budget or eating plan for very long, you are not alone. Willpower is something we all possess in very limited amounts. There's no special gene that gives some people a unique ability to "just say no." Individuals who *seem* more disciplined than others have simply formed deep-seated habits that are serving them well. That is why we spent so much time teaching you the four habits we believe can help you move from knowing *what* to do to actually doing it.

According to experimental social psychologist Roy Baumeister, who has conducted extensive studies on this subject, people have very limited willpower reserves that fail them when they reach what he calls "decision fatigue." In his book *Willpower*, he writes, "People don't realize that decision fatigue helps explain why ordinary sensible people get angry at their colleagues and families, splurge on clothes, buy junk food at the supermarket, and can't resist a car dealer's offer to rustproof their new sedan."[1]

In Dr. Baumeister's "Chocolate Chip Cookie Study," those participants who were presented with a plateful of delicious cookies and asked *not* to eat them before participating in a puzzle exercise gave up quickly in frustration as compared to their counterparts who did not have to exercise such self-control before the challenge.[2] The more often your willpower is tested and you must choose "good" decisions over temptation, the weaker your willpower reserve seems to get. It is almost a use-it-and-lose-it cause and effect. When we've exhausted our ability to resist temptation, most of us default to our autopilot responses, which often include self-indulgence. This is why working on foundational habits is so vital to your long-term success. In order to reduce your exposure to "decision fatigue," consider how you can creatively incorporate one or more of the four habits into the health and wealth advice in this chapter.

Ode to an Unhealthy Lifestyle

I'm a woman on the go, and I'm packing too much stuff.
My purse is overloaded, yet it never holds enough.
Shoes are in abundance, and my closet overflows.
But when there's some place to go, I can't find the right clothes.
What never gets too full to take on added cargo . . .
Are those ever-expanding fat cells turning me into a "lardo."
Days are long and life gets hard, the challenges are whopping,
When stress is high, I seek relief . . . I eat or do some shopping!

WEALTH

66 Learn to manage unintentional spending
by using these helpful tips. **99**

Before marrying Bob, I (Ellie) learned how to use coupons and find sales. I didn't have a financial need because I was a broker making a good living; couponing was just a fun hobby. But it was a different story after we married. I used coupons to feed our family when our income was limited. In fact, I became so good at slashing the prices for groceries that I started offering small seminars to teach others. I realized our family could easily slash monthly expenses in other areas as well: clothing, household goods, and vehicle insurance. All of these little sales and good deals added up to big bucks. I'd become an expert on improving the "out" side of the In and Out Habit, and before we knew it, there was finally more money coming in than there was going out!

A Motivating Reality Check

It's important to conduct your own debt-and-saving-money reality check. For example, realize that if you can save $5,000 a year on the items mentioned above (we save $8,000 on groceries every year—not including the other savings areas), it would be equivalent to earning about $6,800 (by the time you pay taxes and social security). That is an additional $5,000 added to your family—free and clear!

One of the ways we used "saving money" as a way to get out of debt was through a purposeful spending plan. We set up a budget and used the 3D Habit of *determining, delaying,* and *distracting* to help us stick to it and to get out of debt. After years of living debt-free, this is my opinion about debt:

- Debt borrows on your future.
- Debt makes you a servant to the lender.
- Debt places financial stress on you and your family.
- Debt erodes resources through high-interest payments.
- Debt promotes impulse buying.
- Debt limits your ability to be generous.

Our family practiced one other seemingly small thing that also yielded big dividends—we prayed, and that opened a whole new set of positive doors in our lives. We also made other proactive decisions. Despite the fact that Bob's monthly income was locked in, we made a mutual commitment to apply every unexpected check, bonus, or financial gift toward our debt.

Miraculously, there were many unanticipated opportunities to do just that, including:

- USAA insurance premium refund,
- GI Bill reimbursement for Bob's master's program (arrived six years after he finished the program),
- Christmas checks from relatives, and
- military bonus for signing a five-year commitment.

We believe these miracles happened because we were committed to following the habits that would lead us away from debt and toward wealth. While these checks helped pay down our debt, they didn't pay our living expenses. That small miracle occurred on a daily basis because we learned to stretch the value of a dollar. The old saying "Necessity is the mother of invention" was never truer than in the Kay household in those early years.

I developed an ability to save on practically everything a family must purchase by searching for bargains and only buying when the items we really needed were on sale. Here are some of the ways our family used the four Lean Body, Fat Wallet Habits to get out of debt and into financial health:

1. **You Are What You Think Habit:** We stopped spending money because we thought we "deserved" it and changed our self-talk to reinforce that we "deserved" to become debt-free and acquire greater wealth and security. We determined that getting rid of our forty-thousand-dollar debt was important to us and told ourselves that we would make all financial decisions based on this ultimate goal.

2. **The Sustainable Lifestyle Habit:** We set up a budget that was realistic and allowed some room for intentional expenditures that provided fun and recreation—a budget we could live with on a long-term basis. We agreed to evaluate and modify it as necessary so we could live a consistently debt-free lifestyle and still enjoy life.

3. **The 3D Habit:** By reviewing our goals regularly and discussing challenging temptations before we walked into them (like the Nordstrom Half Yearly Sale), we *determined* to keep our primary goal debt reduction. We *distracted* ourselves with budget-friendly activities when temptations were unavoidable and always *delayed* spending money on major purchases until we could determine if they were a good value.

4. **The In and Out Habit:** By being consistently mindful of our budget and monitoring it visually on a regular basis, we made decisions based on an accurate reality check rather than wishful thinking. Paying attention to the details and watching how debt was slowly but surely diminishing reinforced the power of incremental change within this habit. We were aware that what seemed like small, insignificant amounts could add up greatly over time. It was our responsibility to make sure those numbers were adding up in the right direction.

Whatever your challenges are, you can do more than live through them—you can rise above them! Furthermore, if you persevere beyond the problems of today, you will be in a position to be a source of hope to others. Our financial problems became an opportunity to fulfill our destiny of helping others manage their money better. To that end, let us concentrate on some practical ways that the four habits can help you make wise decisions within your budget and get out of debt for life.

Practical Tips for Saving Money

In over twenty years of using coupons, I have saved roughly $160,000 (based on the Cost of Food at Home chart provided by the USDA[3]). I fed our five school-aged children on about $250 a month. This included toiletries, household cleaners, and medicines. It may sound amazing, but you don't have to look any further than reality television to see the value of couponing. You'll find scores of people across the country who are doing the same.

Even after years of being debt-free and having a significantly higher dual-income family than we had when we first got married, I still use coupons. In fact, last year I saved our family of seven over eight thousand dollars by using coupons—and I only spent one and a half hours a week accomplishing this goal. It's easy, if you are organized.

IMPORTANT COUPONING STRATEGY

Always make sure that you are only using coupons for items you actually need and would want even if the coupon was not available. Whenever possible, purchase those items with the coupon when they're on sale. Then you've paid the least price possible. To simplify these matches of sales with coupons, go to CouponMom.com. This way you'll pay even less than you would at discount stores or warehouse clubs.

COUPON APPS AND WEBSITES

Coupon Sherpa and Yowza are great apps to help you find great values at your local store. Download these apps and use them regularly to save 30 percent or more. Both use geographic location or zip codes to target deals at stores near you. You may also want to try the Redlaser app, which can be used to scan the bar code of a product and find out if the item is cheaper somewhere else. As far as websites go, consider using BradsDeals.com or Dealnews.com to get current updates on a variety of bargains.

CLIP EVERY COUPON—SHARE THE SAVINGS

If you don't use a particular product, you can donate that coupon to a "swapbox." It's easy to organize a swapbox at your workplace, club, or church. I've even seen moms get together for "virtual swapbox" play dates with their iPads and smartphones to swap Groupon deals, coupon websites, and other great savings ideas.

To create a swapbox of paper coupons, keep a shoebox-sized container in a central location. You can donate your coupons in a Ziploc bag with a piece of paper in the front called a name card. Write your name and date at the top of the name card and you'll know you donated that bag of coupons. When you look through a bag of coupons, pull out the coupons needed and sign your name to the name card so others know you've benefited from their donations. Groups often assign a "coupon coordinator" to pull expired coupons out of the bags at the end of each month. These expired coupons can be mailed to military units overseas since they're good for six months past the expiration date in commissaries outside the United States. Just e-mail assistant@elliekay. com and put "expired coupons" in the subject line; we will send you a list of bases that could use your donations. Now your friends and family members are also helping military families save money around the world.

PRICE MATCHING—ASK YOUR STORE

If you have a store that will match competitors' ads, then this helps save time and money. Most Walmart stores offer this benefit to their consumers. This price-matching tip is also good outside of the grocery area because there are dozens of other stores that will honor competitors' ads, including Best Buy, Office Depot, Staples, Target, and more. Since these policies vary from year to year (and even month to month), it's important to inquire at the customer service desk before you try to use the price-matching benefit.

To implement this tip, just take in all the local sale ads and have the store match the sale price from the circulars. There may be some restrictions, so be sure you ask for the details at the customer service desk.

For example, Walmart will not honor a "buy one/get one free," nor will they honor "percentage off" sales. But they will substitute their brand for other store brands that are on sale and it may even end up being a better quality deal!

SEARCH HIGH AND LOW FOR BARGAINS

In today's grocery stores, many bargains are located on the top and bottom shelves. The expensive items are at eye level. To those in marketing the reason is obvious—you'll buy something that's in front of your nose! Also, avoid the floral, deli, and bakery departments. They're usually overpriced and can bust your budget.

USE A SHOPPING LIST—DON'T LEAVE HOME WITHOUT IT!

When shopping, you should never leave home without an organized list. It minimizes time spent in the store and helps you stay on target, thus avoiding impulse buying. It can also serve as a reminder of sale prices and coupons you may have. There is an app called Awesome Note, which can be found at Mint.com, that can help you organize a shopping list.

HUNGRY? EAT FIRST OR STAY AT HOME!

Never grocery shop when hungry; you'll be tempted to buy food you don't need. Also, leave small children home whenever possible. It seems like they're always hungry, and they might even try to talk you into buying junk they don't need—take it from a busy mother of seven!

BUY ITEMS ON SALE AND STOCK UP

When you purchase a product on sale, you've usually paid the least price possible for that item. This buying method is different from menu planning. With a specific menu, you're obligated to buy the groceries on your menu. However, when you buy groceries on sale and stock up, you'll have a great selection from which to choose your meal. You've also paid less. So make up your weekly menu according to what you have in your pantry and save more.

SHOPPING ONLINE BARGAINS—LAYER THE SAVINGS!

As part of the "Heroes at Home" world tour, my team of experts and I traveled to various military bases bringing helpful workshops. In this ongoing tour, we visited military members and their families around the world, sharing advice and practical tools on how to cope with the military lifestyle. We also offered money management workshops and taught them how to layer the savings. After our tour, we heard from hundreds of these families who had cut their online expenses in half! Here are three steps to save big online:

Step #1: Use a Shopping Robot. Go to MySimon.com, Amazon .com, or Bing.com for shopping robots that will search the Internet for an item and locate the best deal possible. Once you've finished the first step of finding the best price, you are ready to add the second layer.

Step #2: Use a Coupon Code. Once you've found the best price possible, the second step is to layer in a coupon code. Just go to a code site such as RetailMeNot.com or CouponCabin.com and locate discount codes to save even more. Sometimes these codes are for free shipping, gifts, or percentage discounts. There are also apps such as RetailMeNot that you can use on your smartphone while you are in the store or when shopping online.

Step #3: Use Online Rebates. The final layer is to receive a rebate for your shopping by going to eBates.com or SlickDeals.net. Some of these sites offer referral bonuses for encouraging your friends to sign up for the deals. There are hundreds of participating online sites that offer rebates for your purchases if you take the time to search them out and follow their instructions.

Buying a Car

The least expensive car for you to drive is probably the vehicle you are currently driving! So consider driving that paid-for car a little while longer and taking the money you would spend on a car payment and putting it into a car fund in order to reach the goal of eventually paying cash for your cars.

People talk themselves into a new car for a variety of reasons such as gas mileage. However, when you calculate gas mileage and the money "saved" when compared to interest payments and depreciation on that new car, you will find that you do not even come close to saving money. The average new car depreciates roughly 30 percent within the first eighteen months, with an average loss of value of five thousand dollars as soon as you drive it off the dealer lot. So if it really is time to replace your car, always consider purchasing a used vehicle first.

However, there are occasions when a new car may make sense. For example, when interest rates are incredibly low or your family needs the warranty (because of high mileage for commutes), it may make sense. Try to get an end-of-the-year clearance model or a demonstrator model. If possible, buy the car at the end of September, which is the end of their fiscal year.

The following tips can apply to buying a new or used car, but each sales point should be negotiated separately.

PRICE

Negotiate the price of the car at a dealership apart from the value of the trade-in. Tell the salesperson you want to determine the price of the car without a trade-in. The reason you want to do this is because salespeople will often give you far more for your trade than you expected—thus hooking you on the deal. However, this higher-value-for-the-trade-in shtick can be part of the technique they use to get you to purchase the car. If a higher value is given to the trade, then they will give a lower discount on the price of the vehicle, because all the discounting went into the value of the trade.

TRADE-IN

Now that you've determined the price of the car, ask what the dealer will give you for your trade-in. Most likely, you will get more for your car if you sell it yourself. A little elbow grease and some top-notch detailing can net you hundreds of dollars more than a dealer can give you, if you can find a buyer. Some people (like military families) don't always have the time to sell their car because of moving schedules and so forth. Look up the value of your existing car at Kbb.com or Edmunds.com, print the page, and bring it with you to the car lot to negotiate the price. Not only does Edmunds's car-buying guide list new car prices, used car prices, car comparisons, and car-buying advice, but they also give car ratings, car values, and auto leasing prices. Do the research on the vehicle you are trading in and find out what Kelly Blue Book (Kbb.com) says it is worth. For example, if it is valued at $2,000 and the sales person offers you $3,000 for it, you may want to jump at the deal. But what you may not realize is that the new car you are buying for $20,000 will be discounted $1,000 less simply because they put $2,000 into your trade to get you to jump at the deal. Bottom line: try your best to gather enough facts so that you make a wise decision. Unfortunately, we often see the deal inaccurately as the smell of new leather and gleam of a fresh paint job cloud our sensibilities.

FINANCING

The finance and insurance office is where the lion's share of a dealership's profit is made. In this office, you will have to navigate interest rates, payments, terms, and warranties. Unless you put miles on your car for business or you are purchasing a car that costs a lot to repair (and you intend to keep it longer than the warranty lasts), extended warranties are usually not a good value. We purchased an extended warranty on my Mercedes because it costs so much to repair and we knew we would keep it longer than the warranty lasted. If you do want a warranty, then be prepared to negotiate on the price of the warranty at closing. You can save hundreds, if not a thousand dollars or more on the warranty by negotiating the price.

When it comes to vehicle financing, you can generally do better on interest rates by selecting your own creditor. Unless, of course, the manufacturer is offering a lower APR. The credit life insurance that dealers offer is more expensive than raising your regular insurance premium by twenty thousand dollars to cover this expense.

HEALTH

❝ Learn to manage unintentional eating
by applying four key concepts. **❞**

Just as we need to develop strategies for making wise purchases and saving money, we also need to implement an effective approach to avoid emotional or unintentional eating so we can stop stuffing our fat cells and realize permanent weight loss and better health.

As you've already read, I (Danna) had a major issue with food as a young woman. Yet, even after years of living a healthy, lean lifestyle, I've learned that if I'm not intentional, it becomes easy to relax and forget the In and Out Habit and how small, seemingly insignificant indulgences can add up. So whether you are an out-of-control overeater like I once was, or just a person who has packed on a few excess pounds over many years, this section is for you. Before I share four key concepts that I believe can greatly help, let's recap one of the biggest underlying reasons many people struggle in the area of emotional eating—unhealthy self-talk.

The You Are What You Think Habit and Emotional Eating

This is the most fundamental of the habits and a crucial factor in permanently dealing with emotional eating issues. Since our deep-seated thoughts drive our behaviors, we can be certain that out-of-control behavior is being driven by strong messages you've been telling yourself for a long time. Just as Ellie and her family changed their words and attitudes about spending money so they could move toward a debt-free lifestyle, we also must change our words and attitudes about food if we want to live a fat-reduced lifestyle.

As a young woman, I did not believe that I could control my ability to resist fattening foods. I did not believe I could permanently change my lifestyle or overcome the irresistible urge to eat all day long. I did not believe and, therefore, I did not succeed. Thankfully, we do not need to become servants to our unhealthy thinking permanently. Instead, we can choose to stop indulging our negative thinking (and our appetites). Decide to become acutely aware of your detrimental thoughts, and take them "captive" by refusing to dwell on them. Let the negative thought become a trigger to remind you to replace those thoughts with what you really want and need to believe. This one habit has transformed my life in multiple ways over the years. I consider the time invested in renewing my mind time very well spent.

Personal Temptation Exercise

It is most helpful if you can identify your biggest areas of temptation and the lies associated with those. Then craft an impactful sentence you can use as your new self-talk to replace those lies.

You can add one more "power layer" to this exercise by associating something funny or uplifting with your new message. As mentioned in chapter 2, Shawn Achor's research on positive psychology has demonstrated that we increase our performance and productivity, which can include our ability to exert self-control in a given circumstance, by experiencing something positive before tackling a challenge. This is a great strategy to use before taking a test or engaging in any stressful activity. According to Shawn, even recalling a good memory can make a difference. Get creative and add a little dash of positivity to your new self-talk.

I've included an example of how to approach this exercise below. If you choose to do this exercise later, make sure you take time to come back to this page and complete your homework. Taking action (a subject we'll address more completely in the last chapter) is what will make your hopes and desires become realities.

Here's an example for you to consider:

THE TEMPTATIONS I MOST WANT TO OVERCOME ARE:

I am always tempted to eat junk food. I almost always eat too much at meals. I am especially tempted when I get too hungry, when dining out, or when other people are eating in front of me.

THE LIES I BELIEVE RELATED TO THESE TEMPTATIONS ARE:

I am weak and cannot stop myself from eating foods even though I want to be healthier and lose weight. When foods I like are nearby or others are eating them, I cannot resist them.

THE NEW MESSAGES I WILL USE TO REPLACE THESE LIES ARE:

I believe that I have the power to resist temptations. In fact, junk food and high-calorie snacks are losing their appeal. I crave healthy food and am easily satisfied when I eat.

Positive Power Layer

When I say the words "I've got the power," I laugh at the memory of a song by C&C Music Factory that I used when I taught aerobic exercise classes. I see myself leading a huge group of avid aerobicizers through intense fat-burning routines in our leg warmers, leotards, and sweatbands. When I see foods full of empty calories, I now think of them as a "fat wardrobe" strapped around my thighs and belly (like a doughnut belt). I remind myself of how much better I will look and feel if I just step away from the chocolate cake "jeans."

Your positive power layer doesn't need to be as corny as my example above. Just add a positive or funny image that works for you. The key is to associate something that elicits an upbeat response internally—something that makes you laugh, warmly reminisce, or feel good. I've been helping my sixteen-year-old son develop this technique as I drive him to school in the mornings—especially before a test. I'm teaching him to incorporate this into a habit before a football game, driver's exam, or any other important challenge.

Take Action

The temptations I most want to overcome are:

_____

The lies I believe related to these temptations are:

_____

The new messages I will use to replace these lies are:

_____

Temptation and the 3D Habit

As we've already discussed, the 3D Habit is a great help when you face temptations. One of the keys is to make a habit of implementing it whenever you can *before* you face your challenge. While this is not always possible, much of the time we know the enticements we'll face at places like the movie theater, parties, the break room at work, and even our own refrigerators. Years ago, someone gave me a fridge door magnet with the face of a policeman, and every time someone pulled the door handle, it activated a recording that barked, "Step away from the refrigerator!" Think of the 3D Habit as your internal coach encouraging you with a new message: "You have other options. Step away from this temptation, and do something else instead. You are stronger than this temptation and are *determined* to *delay* this indulgence and *distract* yourself with something that doesn't move you away from your goal."

One of the ways I deal with the temptation of wanting to eat for distraction when I'm engrossed in a long writing project (like this book) is to practice the 3D Habit in the following way. First, I *determine* that I'm not going to eat unless I'm hungry and decide ahead of time what foods I will most enjoy when I finally take a break. Over the years I've realized that this was more difficult to do if I am working from the kitchen table and a bowl of cashews (or some other temptation) is sitting nearby. So I *distract* myself by doing most of my writing upstairs in my office. It's important for emotional eaters to learn to separate the act of eating from work. Because we tend to desire food for reward and comfort more than some people, we cannot fully appreciate it when it's combined with other distracting activities. Ideally, take a break from your work and completely enjoy your meal.

The Happiness Factor author, Shawn Achor, and I have similar ways of approaching the challenge of changing ingrained habits. He shared a story about his attempts to overcome a bad habit of watching too much television. His determination and willpower were not enough. Whenever he returned home exhausted from work, he'd fall into autopilot mode of collapsing on his sofa, grabbing the remote control, and zoning out without even remembering his new resolution. Once he was "down and under the influence," it was hard to reverse his decision. So he essentially practiced what Ellie and I call the 3D Habit in a clever way—he took the batteries out of his remote control! Each time he plopped down and attempted to turn on the TV, he was reminded of his *determination* to change this habit. He said it was amazing how effective a quick disruption in his old habit had become in forming a new one. If you are serious about changing your habits, you need to get creative as well.[4] Find distractions that can work as triggers to remind you to practice your new healthy self-talk and develop new autopilot behaviors that launch you toward your ultimate goals.

Four Key Concepts to Overcome Emotional Eating

As you read and consider the four key concepts that follow, determine to invest a little time in self-evaluation—followed by implementation. As noted in the story about Shawn Achor trying to break his TV habit, we tend to default into the path of least resistance. You will need to summon a bit of your willpower and self-discipline reserves to experiment with some of these concepts. As you practice the four habits, your willpower will be replaced by a new wiring that sends you on a healthier autopilot course. In the meantime, perhaps the following questions will give you a little kick in the tush:

- Is doing what I always do really working for me?
- Do I want to be exactly where I am physically, emotionally, and financially in one year?
- Am I willing to try new things so I can realize my goals?

KEY CONCEPT #1: LEGALIZE FOOD

Let's start with the concept of legalizing food. Most of us have been on more than a few diets in our lives, and most diets deal with restraint and an external control on food. Dieters often believe that certain foods are okay and others are forbidden. This belief creates a struggle and a conflict—a mental tug-of-war. As long as there is a struggle, there is potential for bingeing and eating more than normal. This all-or-nothing attitude is very self-destructive. The minute we tell ourselves we can't have a certain food, we want it more than ever.

Many people take a legalistic stand on foods. They are either "good" or "bad." All foods have caloric value. In other words, they provide energy to the body. If all we eat are empty calories, our bodies are fueled without complete nourishment. Yet, in balance, we can enjoy an occasional dessert or snack just for the pleasure of it.

Many people tell me that they are afraid to make all types of food "legal"—allowing them the choice to eat them rather than putting them on some "forbidden foods" list. They fear that they might choose to eat sweets or junk food all day long. Generally, the opposite happens. When we are too restrictive—eating salads and vegetables and diet foods under restraint—we often end up bingeing out of frustration. It's true that eating junk food from morning to evening is not a balanced diet, but sooner or later, you will crave the healthy foods you need. And when you do, you will eat them. This is because you want them and because you have a choice. At a point, you won't be afraid to make food choices, because you really will believe you are in control. Now, *that* is a healthy attitude.

What Are Your Favorite Foods?

Take a few moments to think about some of your favorite foods. What five things would top your list? You know, the ones you wish had zero calories—the ones that are hard to stop consuming. These are the foods you may try to avoid but find yourself bingeing on when you come face-to-face with them.

1. _____

2. _____

3. _____

4. _____

5. _____

Consider the foods you wrote down. Circle the ones that really seem to take you over the edge. Leave the top three out of this exercise for a few weeks as you build your confidence. Next, choose one or two of the others to test the waters.

Let's say you chose chocolate—sounds good to me! The last thing you want to do is go out and buy a full pound of your favorite caramels and candies. That would be silly. Instead, go to the store or candy shop at the mall and look at all the great choices. Remind yourself that you can have whatever you want. Now choose one small candy bar or two average pieces of chocolate. Put your purchase in a bag, and leave it there until you get home.

Before You Indulge

Make sure you've had a great breakfast and lunch before you treat yourself. Drink a big glass of water and then slowly enjoy your chocolate. Imagine yourself completely satisfied. Tell yourself you are quickly and easily satisfied. This is a self-talk message I gave myself for a full year, and it is now completely true for me. People are amazed that I can eat one-quarter serving of my favorite dessert and leave the rest on my plate. Since you can do this anytime you want, you don't need to feel compelled to indulge more. Tell yourself that message as well! No one has imposed a rule that says you can never eat your favorite foods. It is your choice!

Now go ahead and try to legalize a few foods over the next couple of weeks, being sure you are not rationalizing this exercise into an opportunity to go overboard! Take time to get in touch with how you feel and what you are thinking before, during, and after each "fun food" experience. Record your observations considering the following questions:

- What foods did you eat?
- How did you feel about legalizing them?
- Are there any foods you are afraid to legalize?
- What else did you learn?

Shelving Troublesome Foods

In the quest to overcome emotional eating, you may find that certain foods have a very strong pull on you emotionally. As you work on your self-talk and build your motivational muscles, it may help to put these foods out of reach for a while. Choose safe times when you feel in control to test your ability to eat a small amount of these trigger foods without going overboard. You may use an accountability partner or situation where you will not have an opportunity to access more of your treat than you determined to eat. Keep working on your self-talk until you believe you are in control.

It will take time to establish total comfort in this area. Spend time considering the principles of the You Are What You Eat Habit. Each time you are faced with a food choice, consider the 3D Habit strategy of *determine*, *delay*, and *distract*.

KEY CONCEPT #2: GET IN TUNE WITH YOUR HUNGER

Getting in tune with your hunger is another important element in taking control of emotional eating. Can you tell the difference between physical hunger and emotional hunger? Many of us have lost touch with our natural hunger. What is hunger to you? How does it feel? Do you feel it very often?

It is important to tune in and learn to feed our true hunger with food. Our emotional or "mouth" hunger cannot always be fed every time we get a signal. It's all right to feel hunger. It may seem slightly uncomfortable, but remember, this exercise will help you get in tune with your body's actual physical need for food. No matter how much stored fat you may have, you still have a need to eat every day. So listen to your body when it tells you, "It's time to eat now!"

Your stomach is only about the size of a fist, and it most comfortably holds about two to four cups of solid food at one time. If you eat more than that, it begins to overstretch to accommodate the excess volume. By consistently overfilling your stomach, it gets adjusted to being in an enlarged state. When it is not filled to overfull, you feel falsely hungry. The best way to avoid this dilemma is not to overfill it!

Some interesting studies reveal how smart our bodies are about our need for food. For example, your body knows how many calories you usually burn at certain times during the day. If you eat more than it can use in a given period of time, it almost immediately stores any dietary fat you have eaten. We just can't fool our awesome machines! They know and operate on truth. Therefore, it's important for us to get tuned in to the reality of what we are eating—and why.

The Hunger Scale

By assessing your hunger on a scale from 1 to 5, you can learn to tune in to your eating patterns and ultimately take control over indulging when you are not really hungry. Here is how to rate each number on the scale:

1—I'm absolutely starving! You feel like you could eat anything in sight. You're getting grouchy and shaky, and food is all you can think about. This is when you cave in and eat almost any food within reach and don't care at all about your goals. Avoid this state of hunger—it is very dangerous!

2—I'm hungry. You may feel some twinges or rumbling in your belly. It definitely feels empty, and you're thinking it's time to get some food. This is the time when food actually tastes the best. Have you ever gone out to eat when you weren't hungry and ate just because you were there? It just doesn't taste as good as when your body says it's time to eat. Ideally, you should eat within the hour to avoid moving to a 1 on the scale. It is now that you still have the willpower reserve to choose wisely.

3—I feel neutral. You are neutral at 3: no rumblings, yet no sense of fullness either. It's a very comfortable sensation. But this is the problem: many of us find ourselves eating when we're in this state. Sometimes we eat because the clock says it is time, and at other times because we are receiving an emotional trigger. If you don't feel emptiness at this point, practice the 3D Habit and simply delay eating if at all possible until you move into the 2 range.

4—I'm physically satisfied. Four on the hunger scale means you are physically satisfied. If you are accustomed to overstuffing yourself at meals, it may be challenging to identify that you've had enough to eat. Try to eat very slowly and stop periodically to assess your fullness. Practice ending your meal when you are just a "3+" rather than a four. This will encourage you to eat more frequent small meals, so your body will use your calories more effectively. As you learn to tune in to your hunger, you will identify some new things about your eating patterns. Many of us do not realize how full we are until we get up from the table.

5—I'm "Thanksgiving full"! Being a 5 (absolutely full) only occurs when you have eaten way more food than you need and way more than you can possibly burn for many, many hours. At a 5, you are so stuffed that you need to change into something more comfortable. In fact, you couldn't eat another bite even if someone paid you! But two hours later, you are having a little slice of pie.

Being a 1 or a 5 on the hunger scale should be avoided at all costs. Both are dangerous to your waistline. Getting to 1 on the hunger scale means your body is screaming for sugar. Blood glucose needs to remain at a consistent level for you to feel high energy. When you haven't eaten for a while and your blood glucose starts to dip, your brain's immediate need for sugar overrides all your best intentions and common sense. No matter how much fat you have stored in your reserve tanks, your body thinks it is being starved.

Think about the times you have been a 1 on the hunger scale. When you finally get close to food, how and what do you eat? Most of us will choose anything quick and concentrated in high-fat or high-sugar calories. That is because your brain is screaming, "Sugar, sugar, sugar, now!" Going to a 1 on the hunger scale sets you up for failure. When you finally eat, it usually is much too fast and much too much. Of course, being a 5 on the scale is equally destructive. It means you have eaten way more than your body can process. You know where unburned food goes, don't you? It goes to the exact place you wish it wouldn't. It goes to its favorite retreat on your body—your hips, thighs, or abdomen. Or if you hit a 1 on the scale too frequently, your excess fat will store just about anywhere with no trouble at all!

Hunger Scale Questions to Answer in 7 to 10 Days

1. Are you eating only when you're truly hungry?
2. If not, what are your triggers? Are you bored, angry, tired, or upset?

3. What is your average hunger scale number when you decide to eat?

4. Are you avoiding 1 on the hunger scale?

5. Are you avoiding 5 on the hunger scale?

6. How many times each day are you thinking about food?

7. How many times each day do you eat when you are not hungry?

Remind yourself that you are not on a diet, and there are no forbidden foods. You can eat what you want, when you want it. Since food tastes best when you are truly hungry, choose to wait so you can have maximum enjoyment. When you do decide to eat, think about what will really satisfy you. Is it sweet or sour, smooth or crunchy, spicy, salty, hot, or cold?

In order to get a handle on your eating, it is important to make sure you get both physically and psychologically satisfied when you eat. For the brain to register satisfaction, you need to engage in about fifteen to twenty minutes of eating. The key is to slow down. What is your eating environment like? Are you usually doing something else while you are eating? Do you often find yourself eating standing up? Eating on the run? Fully concentrate on the eating experience. Many times we don't even remember what our food tasted like because we've been talking, reading, or watching television. We have lost the full joy and pleasure of eating.

Naturally Thin Eating

If you've ever lived with a naturally thin person, you may have noticed some key ways they relate to food. Some commonalities include:

- They eat when they are hungry and stop when they are comfortably full.
- They eat what really appeals to them at the time, rather than whatever is convenient.
- They eat slowly and enjoy every bite.
- They forget about food until they are hungry again.

How do *you* develop this kind of healthy eating pattern? Self-discovery and practice, practice, practice.

KEY CONCEPT #3: IDENTIFY YOUR EATING TRIGGERS

Common emotional eating triggers include depression, anxiety, boredom, loneliness, frustration, and feelings of inadequacy. Identify core issues and look for long-term solutions that will reduce or eliminate the emotions that induce nonproductive behaviors.

My Eating Triggers

Rate yourself based on the last six to twelve months as follows:
0—Almost never; 1—Sometimes; 2—Often; 3—Always

_____ When I am frustrated or overwhelmed, eating makes me feel better.

_____ When I am nervous or stressed, eating helps calm me down.

_____ If someone criticizes me or disapproves of me, I often find myself wanting to eat.

_____ Eating soothes me when I feel sad.

_____ Food and eating make things even better when I am very happy.

_____ Some foods I eat make me feel guilty, and then I give up and eat even more.

_____ My anger is reduced when I indulge in foods I like.

_____ If I get in an argument with someone special to me, I feel like eating to ease the pain.

_____ I frequently eat to pass the time when I am bored.

_____ When I feel inferior to someone, I eat to feel better.

_____ I eat more when my life seems too busy or out of control.

_____ When I am mad at myself, I eat more.

_____ When everything seems to be going wrong, I eat to feel better.

_____ I snack a lot while I work, drive, or do certain mundane tasks.

_____ I often eat before I identify any hunger or need to eat.

How Did You Score?

40–45   Poor. Take one step at a time and begin taking action today.

31–39   Fair. It's definitely time to take action and tune in to your emotional eating habits.

22–30   Good. Your thinking is pretty good, but there's room for improvement.

< 21   Excellent! You seem to have a good handle on your emotions and eating habits.

Take Action

If you have many "Often" or "Always" answers, you should spend time tuning in to what is really going on. Sometimes emotional eating is as simple as the fact that you have developed some bad habits. Other times it is an issue of unhealthy self-talk messages overriding all your best attempts. Read your answers again. What do you really believe? Rewrite those messages in a positive way, and say them to yourself daily. Use your new messages to help you change your underlying belief system about your emotional relationship to food.

KEY CONCEPT #4: KEEP A FOOD JOURNAL

A journal is a great tool for measuring progress along a particular path. It can become a self-testing place for personal reflection and inner conversations. Record some of your discoveries in a small spiral notebook you can carry with you. You may want to use your thought notebook that we discussed in chapter 2 for this purpose as well. Include notes about your hunger scale, eating patterns, temptations you face each day, and about how you are using your new habits to change your responses.

Almost everyone eats in response to some kind of emotional arousal at times. If you desire to reduce the frequency of your emotional eating occurrences, identify your eating triggers. A journal will help you keep a record of your behavior and evaluate any common threads. In order to evaluate your eating patterns effectively, it is recommended that you journal your emotional eating for at least seven days.

A typical food diary has an entry for every time something is eaten. It may include:

1. Time of day
2. Type of food eaten
3. Calories and amount of each food
4. Nutritional components (fiber, protein, fat, etc.)
5. Mood at time of eating
6. Hunger Scale before and after eating
7. Place or activities during eating

Once you identify your patterns, it's time to decide what you are going to do about it and start to take action. Remember that you believe what you tell yourself most often. If you want to feel in control of your food choices, you must tell yourself that you are in control—over and over.

The Positive Cycle

One of the most important principles I've learned in overcoming emotional eating is that I always do much better when I'm well rested and my energy level is high. Establish a strong base with a nutritious breakfast and lunch every day. You will be amazed at how many of your cravings diminish when your blood sugar is stable. Your increased energy will prompt you to become more active. Your activity will further increase your energy and decrease your appetite. Taking better care of yourself will give you a sense of well-being that can have a dramatic impact on many of your choices and habits. Soon this positive cycle will dominate your life! I'll share more specific nutrition tips in chapter 8.

As a recovered compulsive eater and bulimic, I know how painful and frustrating emotional eating can be. Please believe me when I say that there is hope! Don't condemn yourself when you succumb to old patterns. Work on changing your perspective and cutting your losses. In years past, I would willfully determine to control my cravings for sweets or junk food. If I finally gave in and had one chocolate chip cookie, it tasted so good that I would have another two or three. After three, I felt so guilty that I ate a dozen more just because I had blown it! The damage didn't come from three or even four cookies. The damage came when I caved in and ate the whole box. And after the first three, they didn't even taste very good.

If you have been struggling with an eating disorder or wondering if you are moving into that arena, it can be helpful to seek professional help. For some people, the unhealthy behavior is only the tip of the iceberg. It is not simply a desperate attempt to avoid weight gain or lose weight more quickly. Many experts say that bulimia and anorexia are behaviors that demonstrate the individual's desperate need to take control of his or her life. No matter what, don't do what I did and hide your struggle. That will only make things worse. Share your concerns with a safe and wise person. Ask a trusted friend or mentor to give you guidance. There are programs such as Remuda Ranch (RemudaRanch.com) that have been successfully helping people with severe eating disorders for many years.

Whether you seek professional help or not, you will greatly benefit from changing your unhealthy thinking. In fact, professionals call this "cognitive therapy," and it is widely accepted in both faith-based and secular therapy. It took time for me to change those old thinking patterns.

It took time to believe I could be in control. Today I can eat a little more than I should and then stop and say, "Hey, that tasted great! Now I'll just have to burn a few more calories and eat lighter at dinner." You know what? It works! Today I know I am in control of my food choices. I also know you are in control of yours. Soon you will know it too!

8.

Healthy Investments for Body and Bank

*Have a healthy and wealthy future by making
the right investments consistently.*

The room was packed with three hundred women who were excitedly anticipating their long-awaited weekend retreat in the mountains of California. They had just settled back in their chairs and were listening to the emcee briefly share a few tidbits about their speaker for the weekend—me (Danna). As I stepped on the stage, I knew that they would all do what women naturally do: assess me from head to toe and register their first impression before I even spoke a word. So, in order to be transparent and tell them what they were all wondering anyway, I stepped onto the stage and said, "Life flies by amazingly fast, doesn't it? In fact, I can hardly believe that in three months, four days, and three hours (but who's counting?)"—long pause—"I will be sixty years old." I said nothing more, because they were not listening. There was a buzz in the room as the women murmured to each other. Later, I discovered that some of them thought I was lying. Others assumed I'd had lots of "work" done and wanted the name of my plastic surgeon!

Today I am pushing toward my sixty-first birthday. Like most mature women, I am keenly aware of the pull of gravity and the feeling that time is being fast-forwarded. Yet, something contradictory is happening as well. I am reaping some very positive rewards—almost defying my age because of the long-term investments I've consistently made in my health over the last three decades.

Even my husband, Lew, admits that I look younger than I did ten years ago. He made a sweet comment to me not long ago. "Love, it is really pretty amazing," he said. "Here I am seven years younger than you—and most people think I'm seven years *older*. I think you should share whatever it is you're doing with other women. I'm really blessed to be growing *old* with you as you seem to actually be growing *young*!"

Small Investments Add Up in Big Ways

I (Ellie) have almost raised my seven children and consider my life as a mom to be my greatest role. I was able to break through in the marketplace as the original coupon queen, publishing the best-selling book *Shop, Save and Share*, when my youngest children were three, five, seven, nine, and eleven. That was fourteen years and fifteen books ago. Today my expertise has expanded to include all aspects of personal finance. I'm known as "America's Family Financial Expert" and have shared my advice on over eight hundred television and radio stations around the world.

I started with the simple habit of clipping coupons for my family, and now, over the course of twenty years, those coupons have saved us over $160,000. I taught my children the financial skill of a good work ethic and followed my own advice when it came to preparing them for college. To date, my family has cashed in on over 1.5 million dollars in college scholarships, and the Kay kids are garnering five college degrees that are completely debt-free.

The little things, whether couponing or child training, can add up to pay huge dividends. And that doesn't include accumulating interest on 401(k)s, SEPs, TSPs, 529 plans, and other kinds of investments that grow over time. The bottom line is that the financial investments our family made have paid off in huge ways and will continue to reap a harvest for many generations to come.

Reaping health and wealth rewards both now and in the future happens only when we make consistently wise investments. If we live only for today, our quality of life tomorrow will be greatly diminished. We believe that you can find a balance of enjoying today while investing for the future both physically and financially. In this chapter, we will share important principles and practical tips for making investments that will result in long-term rewards.

HEALTH

66 You can have a healthy future . . . if you make the right physical investments consistently. **99**

In 1970 at age eighteen, I (Danna) bought my first car with my life savings of four hundred dollars. It was a 1949 Volkswagen Beetle with an oxidized green paint that made me look like I was driving around town in an old army helmet. Can you imagine if that was the only car I would drive for my entire life? Fortunately for me, I've owned many other cars over the last forty-two years!

Your Body—Your Vehicle for Life

Unlike the cars we purchase one year and then sell or trade in the next, our bodies are our one and only vehicle for life. No matter what condition it is in, or how we'd love to get a new one, this is it, folks! It makes sense to take good care of our precious equipment. When we don't feel well, it impacts our entire day and attitude. Even a small headache, lack of sleep, or sour stomach can hold us back from looking, feeling, and doing our best. Despite this fact, many of us treat our bodies with less care than we do our cars. I'm not pointing any fingers here. Remember, I'm the gal who took diet pills, binged and purged five times a day, and strived like a workaholic for eight years of my life. Thankfully, I learned before the damage was irreversible how crucial my health is to the quality of my life.

The 70/30 Rule

Some people live on excuses like, "I can't help that I'm fat; my whole family is fat" or "Why eat healthfully? My mother was a health fanatic and died at forty from cancer." About 30 percent of our physicality is out of our control. We can have genetic predispositions to certain diseases and other physical issues; however, they do not condemn us to the worst possible outcome. Similarly, we are influenced by our hormones—male or female. They are mostly out of our control as well—just ask any menopausal woman—and will sometimes be the root for some various health challenges.

What most people fail to focus on is this positive reality: we have 70 percent control over our health and wellness. It's called our *lifestyle*. How we choose to eat, exercise, sleep, relax, think, and deal with stress is predominantly up to us. By taking positive action over what you *can* control and maximizing your health, you can greatly diminish the downside of the 30 percent you cannot. When you take personal responsibility, the vehicle you've got a lifetime lease on will serve you well. Hopefully, you'll drive it for so long that you'll need to negotiate with the Manufacturer about the excess miles!

Essential Health Investments

While there are many important health principles and practices we could discuss about investing in your long-term health, I want to emphasize four obvious, yet often poorly implemented, essentials that can vitally impact your wellness both now and for many years to come. They are the following:

- Exercise
- Nutrition
- Sleep
- Recreation and Relaxation

HEALTH INVESTMENT #1: EXERCISE

It's true what they say: "If you don't use it, you'll lose it." When it comes to your body, you can actually begin losing muscle on a microscopic level within forty-eight to seventy-two hours if you don't work out frequently. The older we get, the faster we lose it. Yet those who stay active can not only lose weight and increase energy but also realize some pretty dramatic anti-aging benefits as well.

We frequently make the excuse that we don't have time to fit exercise into our lives. But the short- and long-term benefits of a consistently active lifestyle are simply too good to miss! If I haven't convinced you yet, here are a few more important reminders of why you need to invest in daily exercise. Exercise

- controls weight,
- improves mood,
- boosts energy,
- promotes better sleep,
- improves your sex life, and
- relaxes and reenergizes.

Exercise also combats health conditions and diseases and gives you a lower risk of

- coronary heart disease and stroke,
- type 2 diabetes,
- colon cancer,
- breast cancer,
- early death,
- osteoarthritis,
- depression, and
- dementia.

In addition, regular exercise tends to promote healthier choices in other areas of your life. Stop believing the lie that you don't have time to exercise. The truth is that you can't afford *not* to! In the next chapter, I'll share how exercise can de-stress you as well.

> When God created humans, He also provided all the nutrients we needed to maintain a healthy body. He did not hide those nutrients from us, and He didn't package them separately and write a book to explain exactly how each one functions. He simply put an abundance of nutrients in the foods that we would eat.
>
> —James Balch, MD

HEALTH INVESTMENT #2: NUTRITION

It sounds cliché, but you really are what you eat. God has created our bodies with blueprints and programs to make new cells in every part of our bodies. It is our job to give our bodies the building materials to generate high-quality replacement parts. Skin and blood cells regenerate very quickly and our skeletal systems very slowly. But within seven years every single cell in your body will be different from what you have this very moment. My question to you is this: what quality will that new body be? It will depend on the foods you eat (or don't eat) every single day. If you simply improve the quality of your nutrition 10 to 20 percent in the next year, your body will respond in remarkable ways.

Eating to build the best new body possible is not very complicated. For most of us, it means decreasing empty calories and adding more nutrient-dense foods to our daily diet. With that in mind, I will share five important nutritional elements that can help you increase your energy and build healthy new cells every day.

Water

Second only to air, your body must have a constant supply of water to survive. Most people die of dehydration within a few days without it. Your body doesn't sweat soda or iced tea; it sweats water and electro-lytes. It needs water to perform all of its bodily functions, and when you don't drink enough, it resorts to handling only the most essential func-tions. Many people live with chronic low-grade dehydration resulting in a variety of negative outcomes, such as low energy, poor skin tone, and inadequate fat metabolism, to name a few. Try to drink at least four to eight ounces of water for every hour you are awake. If you wait to drink it until you're thirsty, you're already at least one quart low. If you want to look younger, have more energy, and live longer, then drink pure, fresh water all day long. This is an essential habit for good health.

Plant Foods

Fiber-rich fruits, vegetables, whole grains, beans, legumes, seeds, and nuts are packed with vitamins, minerals, phytochemicals, antioxidants, and fiber that help fight cancer, provide anti-aging protection, and more. Study after study shows increasing evidence that this area of nutrition will have the most profound long-term effect on your health and vitality.

Supplements cannot completely fill in the gaps left from not eating enough whole foods. The fiber alone in plant foods has an incredible bal-ancing effect on blood sugar. By eating at least five to ten grams of fiber-rich foods at every meal, you will stay full longer and have more energy. High fiber also greatly benefits your entire digestive system. And don't forget that your breads and cereals should have enough whole grains to be considered a complete food. Look for at least three to six grams of fiber in cereals and two to four grams in breads. Most refined, packaged foods enter the body and are turned into sugar and paste within minutes of ingestion. No wonder we can feel sluggish after we eat too many empty calories.

Another important reason to increase your plant food intake is to bring your body back into the right acid/alkaline balance. When we are too acidic from eating foods like protein, sugar, coffee, and carbonated beverages, our bodies become inflamed and more susceptible to illness. Only plant foods can counteract this acid and diminish those ill effects. The problem is that the American diet is extremely low in plant foods. When we are balanced, our energy increases, it is easier to lose weight, and our overall health soars. I will teach more extensively on this subject later in this chapter.

Quality Protein

Protein is essential for tissue repair, maintenance, and growth of muscles, blood, hormones, enzymes, and antibodies. You should always eat some protein with breakfast and lunch, because like fiber, it digests very slowly and stabilizes your blood sugar. A stable blood sugar promotes higher energy and diminishes hunger. However, more is not always better. Too much protein can tax your body, particularly wreaking havoc on your kidneys. There is no healthful evidence to validate the outrageous propensity toward high-protein diets. Why did God create such an incredible array of colorful foods for us to eat if we were designed to be predominately carnivores?

For now, try to get at least twelve to fourteen grams of protein at both breakfast and lunch. Also, find creative ways to add protein to your snacks, such as nuts or peanut butter on whole-grain crackers. Protein at dinner is not nearly as important as earlier in the day. I know this runs contrary to American customs, but at the very least, we would do well to eat at least half our usual portion in the evening.

Healthy Fats

Choosing the right fats and understanding their benefits and drawbacks will help you dramatically in your weight-management efforts. Keeping the right amount of healthy fat in your diet will leave you feeling full and satisfied longer than a nonfat meal. Fats have long been getting a bad rap, but the truth is that some are essential to your health. The key is to eat the right kind because, as with carbohydrates, not all fats are created equal. Lots of people simply eat too much fat. But many more get almost none of the vitally essential omega-3 fatty acids that have a crucial impact on our health. This essential fat dramatically impacts brain function and cardiac health and has been linked to positive protection from Alzheimer's disease. It is also an incredible beauty aid as it provides the vital nutrients to promote healthy skin.

For now, try to reduce the saturated (animal and dairy) fats as much as possible. The total fat in your diet should range between 15 and 30 percent. Stay on the lower end until you reach your ideal size. Olive oil is always a good choice for cooking and salads. Or try adding omega-3 fats to your diet by eating cold-water fish like salmon and tuna at least two times per week. Walnuts and flaxseed are also very high in omega-3 fat.

Unfortunately, due to pollution, heavy metals like mercury have contaminated fish all over the world. Salmon is actually the only food that can give you an adequate supply of omega-3 nutrition in one six-ounce serving. But if you eat salmon every day, you'll glow in the dark. The sad reality is that we must all supplement this vital nutrient. I have been taking it for about five years, and my skin is better than it was in my forties. If that's not motivation enough, I know I'm going to have a healthier brain as I replace all my worn-out gray matter cells day after day.

Supplementation

Vitamins and minerals are nutrients that occur naturally in foods and are essential for health, yet provide no calories. Antioxidants are a specific group of nutrients that form an army to capture metabolic waste products called free radicals and transport them out of the body before they can damage the cells. All these micronutrients act like spark plugs, working to help the body do its various functions effectively. They also help us more effectively utilize our food as fuel and prevent nutritional deficiencies.

God provides all the nutrients we need in natural foods. The problem is that we don't eat the amount and variety of whole foods necessary to meet all of our nutritional needs. We also have corrupted our natural food sources with depleted soil, polluted water, and chemical agents like pesticides. Today it's important to take vitamins and minerals as an insurance policy. However, they do not take the place of healthy eating. New spark plugs won't make your car run better if you forget to put gasoline in your car. And vitamins without good food are of little value.

If you're not already taking vitamins, start with a good multivitamin mineral complex and an antioxidant formula. Then, if you have a specific need, supplement based on the recommendations of your health-care professional. A word of wisdom: don't spend a fortune on micromanaging your nutrition before you get the basics down. Keep in mind that taking supplements alone does not take the place of implementing the four Lean Body, Fat Wallet Habits!

Eating healthfully and exercising are essential building blocks for good health and a lean body. But we also need to take a quick peek at some of the things we are putting in our mouths that are potentially robbing us of our good investments.

Many of our foods have become so processed, preserved and full of chemicals that they are hardly foods at all, but rather manufactured products that happen to be somewhat digestible.
—Dr. Francisco Contreras

Pick Your Poisons
If you could see the direct impact that some foods you eat have on the cells of your body and realize the negative potential, you'd probably

eat them anyway. Why? Because they taste so good. Most of us feel like we're being punished if we don't indulge our taste buds with our favorite foods. But when we do this on a daily basis, our bodies respond with excess weight, decreased immunity, increased disease, and low energy. You'd think we'd care more, but immediate, delectable gratification is a pesky, little devil—and that's why we're writing this book! Knowing is not enough. So as you read why some of the things you love so much are bad for your body, keep in mind that the four habits we've given you can help you change your mind, determine a new path, evaluate the in-versus-out value, and create a sustainable lifestyle where you can indulge in small amounts and be fully satisfied!

Try a New Perspective on Empty Calories

If someone told you that there was arsenic in the plate of brownies on the table, you'd definitely avoid them. But if it was just a teeny little bit that wouldn't make you feel sick or die, and these brownies were the only chocolate dessert on the planet . . . you might consider just a bite. In essence, we are slowly poisoning ourselves by constantly indulging in empty-calorie foods that are robbing our health and vitality. Don't get me wrong. I'm far from a purist. I do enjoy a small ration of empty calories, but I have learned the value of consistent moderation and reaped the greater reward.

Enjoying a food just because it tastes good can be done in moderation if we don't rationalize what moderation really is. Each year that I research and teach about this topic, I have a harder time indulging with joy. I simply cannot eat some things with reckless abandon anymore. Not because they are fattening, but because they are unhealthy. All the facts just keep ricocheting off the walls of my brain and tormenting me if I start to go overboard. That may seem like a foreign concept to some of you, but it is a great freedom to move from craving foods that have no value to having little or no interest.

It is my personal rule to save any empty "fun food" choices until after lunch if I'm going to allow myself to indulge. But I broke that rule awhile back and ate a doughnut someone offered me and paid the price. As my energy hit the floor, I kept thinking, *It didn't taste good enough to feel this tired an hour later.* It was a good reminder of why I don't make that choice very often.

Because of my years of healthy self-talk, I'm easily satisfied without feeling legalistic or overly restrictive. If someone serves dessert, I will eat a portion of it. If a friend wants to share a slice of pie, I might eat a third of it. Because I know that I can have anything I want anytime I want it, I rarely crave it. I crave a healthy, high-energy body more. I share all this to illustrate how seeing each bite you take for what it really is can change your attraction to it. By deciding to think differently about the foods that can do you harm, you won't feel as compelled to eat them. With all this in mind, I'd like to give you a few motivating facts about several hazardous ingredients found in many of our favorite indulgences.

Hazardous Substance #1: Sugar. Sugar tastes good to your taste buds and acts badly in your body. It simply is not good for you. Sucrose, fructose, lactose, raw, confectioners, or "natural" sugar may have some minor differences, but all metabolize similarly in your body. Though your brain needs a constant supply of glucose (blood sugar) to survive, it doesn't need it in such a simple form. Our bodies are great at converting any kind of food to glucose in order to provide an ample supply to our brains. Excess sugar reacts with proteins in the body and produces a damaging effect similar to free radicals. It promotes aging, decreases your immunity, promotes weight gain, and increases your incidence of diseases like diabetes.

Hazardous Substance #2: White Flour. Refined bread products, white-flour pastas, crackers, and the like convert very quickly to sugar. In fact, if you put a piece of white bread in your mouth for a few minutes, you will notice a sweet taste. The starch is converting to glucose. Yes, your white bread is fortified with important vitamins and minerals, such as iron and folic acid, and contains a smidgen of protein and fiber. But for the most part, refined carbohydrates are sweet nothings. Think of it this way: every slice of white bread you eat is a bit like eating three or four vitamin-fortified marshmallows. A cup of pasta equals eight marshmallows.

Hazardous Substance #3: Bad Fat. If you were to get your blood drawn right after a fatty meal, you would be horrified. Sometimes you can actually see the fat in the tube of blood as it comes out of your vein! I wish that God had given us personal scopes to see what was happening microscopically inside our bodies moment to moment. I truly believe it would motivate us to stop doing some things and start doing others. The point is that most of us are eating way too much saturated and trans fat. All those years we were eating margarine and thinking we were doing the right thing, we were actually deceiving ourselves. As it turns out, when vegetable oil is hydrogenated to be solid at room temperature, it produces trans fats that act much like saturated fats. The problem is that we are getting unhealthy fat from a multitude of sources. The obvious source is meat and dairy products. But much of the fat is hidden in our packaged foods. Become a "fat" detective and start getting some of that sludge out of your diet today!

Hazardous Substance #4: Artificial Sweeteners. Saving calories any way we can sounds like a noble quest. Yet using artificial sweeteners on a regular basis sets you up for some possible health issues that could easily be avoided. While sugar and white flour are empty calories that create problems when taken in excess, artificial sweeteners are chemicals (despite their "natural" origins) that your body cannot always effectively expel. The most widely known artificial sweeteners are aspartame and saccharin. You'll find these in diet foods like frozen desserts, soft drinks, chewing gum, gelatin, no-sugar-added baked goods, and tabletop sweeteners. Many studies are showing that these products actually increase our sugar cravings. Many studies over the past several decades have led most experts to conclude that eating saccharin actually increases rather than decreases the single most reliable predictor of weight gain. Despite sugar's downside, most nutritionists recommend using small amount of it over artificial products.

HEALTH INVESTMENT #3: SLEEP

Sleep plays a much more important role in our health than people have previously realized. It is the time when you get both physical and psychological rest. During deep (REM) sleep, your body accomplishes its most important cellular renewal. Even modest amounts of sleep deprivation can diminish your immune system and ability to cope with the daily challenges of life. If you want to look younger, feel better, and live longer—get enough sleep! How much is enough? Experts suggest that most people need close to eight hours of sleep every night.

I have found that chronic fatigue is one of the biggest factors impacting emotional eating, a lack of desire to exercise, and one's ability to cope with the normal stresses of everyday life. Add an extreme life challenge into the mix, and a sleep-deprived person may totally "lose it." When we don't get enough sleep, our bodies seek to find another source of energy, and we often are drawn to sugar and other empty calories to make up for it. Make sleep a priority. Try getting eight hours of sleep a night for a full month and see the impact it makes in your lifestyle.

Here are a few basic but important tips for improving your sleep habit:

1. Try to establish and maintain a regular time for going to bed.
2. Design a winding-down plan the hour before bedtime, such as a hot shower or bath, a cup of herbal tea, and dimming the lights.
3. Turn off the television and read things that do not get your heart pumping.
4. Take some slow, deep breaths as you relax into bed and

determine not to rehash the challenges of the day. Many people find that taking ten minutes to plan and prioritize tomorrow helps them let go and relax.

5. If you are pushing forty or more years old, consider taking a melatonin supplement. As we get older, this hormone that helps us relax diminishes and sleep decreases. Melatonin also has some anti-aging properties. I take it every night!

6. If you have enough room in your "calorie bank account," a small amount of carbohydrates before bed can increase your feel-good hormone, serotonin, and help you relax. I often have two graham crackers with natural peanut butter and herbal tea before bed.

HEALTH INVESTMENT #4: RECREATION AND RELAXATION

It is difficult for some people to relax. Whether you're type A like me and it is part of your DNA, or you are simply too busy, we all need downtime. The busier and more stressed we are, the more we need to relax. In the next chapter, we'll specifically address the health issues related to prolonged stress and how it impacts not only your emotions but also your body as well. I will give you specific ways to decrease your emotional and physical sense of stress, and Ellie will give you lots of ways to put some fun back into your life without breaking your budget. No matter what your current situation is, it's important to realize that we need a few moments in every day and longer moments in each week to simply unwind and nurture ourselves.

Years ago, I read a poem that has been posted and e-mailed around the world by many people. The author is unknown, but it tells of a person's dream in which he gets an opportunity to interview God. The first question he asks God is, "What surprises you most about humankind?" God's answer resonated with me at the time because I was on a journey to lead a more balanced life. Perhaps these few excerpted verses will speak to you as well and encourage those of you who rarely take time for recreation and relaxation, to do just that!

God answered:

That they get bored with childhood,
rush to grow up, and then
long to be children again.
That they lose their health to make money . . .
and then lose their money to restore their health.
That by thinking anxiously about the future,
they forget the present, such that they live in neither
the present nor the future.
That they live as if they will never die,
and die as though they had never lived.

INVESTING FOR A LONG, HEALTHY LIFE

In an interesting book called *The Immortality Edge* about the science of extending life, the authors write about the "secrets of your telomeres for a longer, healthier life."[1] Telomeres? I never realized I had them—but I do—and so do you! Read on and don't get distracted by the strange word *telomere* because there's a wonderful payoff at the end, especially if you are beyond midlife!

Telomeres are defined as the segments of DNA at the ends of chromosomes that break off and grow shorter and shorter as the cell reproduces. When the telomere reaches its critical limit, the cell either stops reproducing or dies. Infants have very long telomeres, and adults have shorter ones. The authors say that telomere biology is "an extension of all other theories on aging—including wear and tear, antioxidant deficiency, and all sorts of other deterioration theories."[2] Why am I telling you this? Because discoveries have been made that are causing many scientists to believe we can not only stop aging but reverse it. Wow!

I flipped through this interesting book to look beyond the pure science and theory to find out what I could do *today* about those little telomeres that were shrinking daily as my cells replicate into an imperfect replica of my younger self. I realized that I have already been doing most of the things that keep my telomeres long and strong.

Here are my top ten lifestyle factors that helped me score highly on the "Telomere Test." And it is no surprise that we've already addressed most of them! Now you can invest for the future and keep *your* little DNA tails nice and long.

1. Sleep seven to nine hours most nights.
2. Take omega-3 supplements every day.
3. Exercise six to seven days a week.
4. Deal with your stress through healthy thinking and habits.
5. Love life—attitude is almost everything.
6. Take supplements to fill in your nutritional gaps.
7. Eat at least thirty grams of fiber every day.
8. Use olive oil instead of other vegetable oils.
9. Drink green tea (or supplements).
10. Never overeat.

WEALTH

❝ You can have a wealthy future . . . if you make the right financial investments consistently. **❞**

Five Principles for Wise Financial Investments

If you want to reach your investment goals, then it's important to start somewhere. Oftentimes, I've (Ellie) found that people procrastinate working on investments because it seems too complicated or difficult to pursue. Others will sometimes feel that they don't have enough money to begin to invest. Consequently, I recommend that you start where you are and do what you can and learn to look at investments differently. The only real failure is to continue to procrastinate or do nothing at all to work on this area of your money matters. Here are five principles for wise financial investments that are a good place to begin.

INVESTING PRINCIPLE #1: CONSIDER EVERY PURCHASE AS AN INVESTMENT

In the sixth grade, I went to Spain to spend the summer with my Spanish cousins and took three rolls of film with me. I was such a saver that I came back having used only half of one roll. I "saved" two and a half rolls of film and was proud of myself. But I missed the point. Instead of taking pictures of the Alhambra in Granada, the gorgeous beaches on the Mediterranean Sea, the Rock of Gibraltar, and the Almudena Cathedral in Madrid, I kept the camera in my pocket, determined not to "spend" film but to save it. How foolish.

The young and inexperienced girl who spent that summer in Spain has grown up to be a penny-pinching mama who has to step back and reevaluate what it means to spend money. As I practice the 3D Habit before I purchase an item, I need to realize that even after I *determine, distract,* and *delay,* it still might be wise to purchase a quality item.

I've learned that cheaper isn't always better. For example, when I had five babies in seven years, I made it a practice to take care of my health by exercising five times a week. This meant that I had to take all the kids with me, and it required that we purchase a double stroller. Bob wanted to buy quality that would handle the twenty miles a week I put on those stroller wheels, but I wanted to buy cheap. Bob figured that along the lines of the In and Out Habit, we would get a longer life out of a better initial investment. But I was determined to go the inexpensive route. Unfortunately, I learned that cheap was a bad investment because the cheap stroller broke. Did I learn my lesson after the first double stroller purchase? No; I bought cheap a second time and a third. The bottom line was that we ended up buying three double strollers and spent more money than if we had purchased one high-quality stroller in the first place.

Look at all your purchases as if they are investments. Practice the

3D Habit to avoid impulse buys, but also consider the In and Out Habit when it comes to getting your money's worth out of the quality of the item. Here are some areas to get you thinking about when it's important to invest now in order to save later.

Programmable Thermostat (invest $50): One of these is easy to install and should save you around $250 a year on home energy costs.

Laptop Computer Warranty (invest $100+): Whether you are buying an Apple plan or a warranty from Best Buy, it's important to invest in your investment. Laptops cost more to service than desktops, and they often cost more to replace. If you have a nice laptop that you use daily or for work, then it's wise to get the extended warranty.

Mortgage Refinance (closing costs vary): I've worked with a lot of families who have decent credit scores but don't want to go through the hassle and uncertainty of a mortgage refinance. When they use my tools at EllieKay.com and see that they can shave years off the mortgage and reduce their monthly payments, they often decide it is good to invest in a refinance now in order to reap the long-term benefits later. If you can get at least one full percentage point lower than the interest rate you're now paying, then go for it. Just make sure that you crunch the numbers, using the tool called "Loan Payment Calculator with Amortization Schedule" listed under the "Mortgage" tools at EllieKay.com, and be sure you shop around for different lenders.

Energy Star Appliances: Energy Star appliances promise to save you 40 percent on energy and water bills but sometimes cost 70 percent more than non–Energy Star certified. This can be a great example of the In and Out Habit of investing now to save later. For example, if you have an older, top-loading washing machine, it costs around $44 per year in energy. An Energy Star–rated front loader costs only $18 per year in energy (gas or electricity). But it also saves 40 percent on water, uses less detergent, and the clothes come out less damp, which means less time in the dryer. All these additional savings, including the savings of around seven thousand gallons of water for an average-sized family, mean that this is a good investment. Go to EnergySavers.gov to find a list of appliance rebates and tax credits that may be available for Energy Star–rated appliances in your state.

Health Insurance: Be sure to consider how much you pay for health insurance an investment as well. With the new health insurance exchanges you will be able to comparison shop for affordable health plans by going to Healthcare.gov. Companies like WellPoint, who's local affiliated plans are often known as Anthem Blue Cross and Blue Shield, are creating tools to help make choosing the right plan simple. For instance, Anthem and its sister plans will offer family checklists that provide consumers simple steps to select the right health plan as well as a subsidy estimator to help families navigate their financial options.

INVESTING PRINCIPLE #2: CARE FOR LONG-TERM SAVINGS: 401(K), TSP, SEP, OR FIA

The 401(k), which has long been known as the ticket to retirement for millions of Americans, is under attack from within. Many retirement savings options have taken a hit in recent years. For example, when companies lowered the matching portion of 401(k) plans, many workers got disgruntled and stopped contributing. I believe you can have a nice retirement if you take the steps to take care of your retirement account whether you are investing in a 401(k) or a Thrift Savings Plan (TSP—for military and civilian government employees), or whether you are a small business owner and fund your own SEP (Simplified Employee Pension). As an author and speaker, I fund an SEP for myself while my husband has a 401(k) at work and my military sons contribute to TSPs while serving in the military. These accounts are prime examples of how effective the In and Out Habit can be as you invest today to yield tomorrow's retirement income. But make sure you follow the Sustainable Lifestyle Habit and that you contribute enough to make a difference, but not so much that you can't keep up the pace.

Fund It

So what if your company used to match 100 percent of a certain amount you contribute and now they only match 15 to 25 percent?

You aren't going to get that kind of a return through other investments! Certainly 15 to 25 percent is better than nothing at all. Plus, all these accounts offer a long-term, tax-favored status that will pay off in the long run if you put money into the account. Set this up on an automatic allotment so it comes out of the first part of your paycheck or profits.

Forget Borrowing from It!

In recent years, record numbers of participants in 401(k) plans took hardship withdrawals from their savings. Additionally, 45 percent of participants who took those hardship withdrawals also took another one in the same year. Under IRS guidelines, 401(k) administrators can grant hardship withdrawals only for specific reasons, including tuition payments, the purchase of a primary residence, unreimbursed medical bills, and prevention of foreclosure. The majority of those who borrowed to save their homes from foreclosure ended up with foreclosed homes anyway, plus they lost most of their retirement. The long-term impact of raiding your 401(k) is devastating because of possible penalties, taxes, and the lost opportunity cost for your money to grow.

Feel Free to Roll Over Your Fund

Are you getting ready to change jobs or retire? Maybe your employer has decided to end your traditional pension (defined benefit) plan. Whatever the case may be, you have an important decision to make—what to do with your retirement savings. You can roll it into an IRA or into your new company's 401(k) plan. This can be complicated and depends on your age, the possibility of comingled funds, whether you are vested in your previous company, and if you want a trustee-to-trustee rollover.

It's a good idea to contact a fund manager who is known to have low fees so that you can keep more of your retirement money and still get the advice you need for your situation. Vanguard.com or TDWaterhouse .com are good options if you want to open an IRA to roll over your

401(k). You will need to choose your funds and roll them over as the old plan sends the assets to the new IRA fund. If you want to consider this option, be sure to get a statement from your current plan as well as what your plan needs to release the money.

Fixed Indexed Annuities

Savvy and conscientious consumers looking for smart solutions and control of their long-term finances during uncertain times recognize the important role that fixed indexed annuities play in any balanced financial plan. That's because FIAs provide protection from stock market volatility, guaranteed interest and income, and the opportunity for additional interest when markets are up. Go to www.IndexedAnnuitiesInsights.com for tips on what kind of FIA will work best for your portfolio.

INVESTING PRINCIPLE #3: MAXIMIZE SHORT-TERM INVESTMENTS

It's just as important to know what *not* to do with your money as it is to know what *to do* with that savings. If you are like most savers, you're saving for the short term—at least temporarily. So that means you should not tie up your investments in stocks. If in the next three to five years, you plan on starting a business, buying a home, sending a child to college, or buying a car, you should look at short-term investing and not long term. There is a difference between funding long-term investments, such as retirement, and saving cash that you might need in the next three to five years. You should not put these short-term investments into money market accounts or traditional CDs because the money sitting in these low-yield accounts, when weighed against inflation, are basically making you nothing. When you do the math, you'll see that a basic account making around 1.7 percent interest, after you pay taxes on the growth and then adjust for a 2.5 percent inflation rate, is losing you money. In fact, that $100 you now have could be worth $98.60 next year. Here are some options for good returns on short-term investments:

High-Interest-Bearing Checking

These checking accounts are a good place to start. In the past, these kinds of checking accounts haven't been worth the effort. But recently, some financial companies have responded to the economic situation and have found a way to still make money by allowing you to earn money as well. These kinds of high-interest-bearing checking accounts can usually be found in small- to medium-sized banks, and some of them are paying 4 percent interest, which is thirty times what you could make in an average checking account or money market account. You can go to CheckingFinder.com to find one of these kinds of accounts. There is a catch, however: you must follow their rules for debit card use, automatic payments, and any other restrictions.

Nontraditional Certificates of Deposits

First, look for the introductory teaser rates, which are found at Bankrate.com or Ratebrain.com. You've seen the teaser rates for credit cards, and these are basically the same kind of offer—they have limitations and stipulations, and if you want them to work for you, then you'd better know what those boundaries are. Most of these introductory CD rates are from banks that want to boost their deposits by offering a gorgeous interest rate. As long as they are FDIC insured, you don't have to worry.

Step-Up CD

This is another nontraditional CD that offers longer maturing CDs at a higher rate for each year that you hold the certificate. For example, the first year it may offer a 1 percent return, but in years two and three, you could see it rise to 2 percent, and in the fourth and fifth years, it would be 4 percent. They are FDIC insured, and you will need to buy them through your brokerage firm. But the good news is that you do not pay the commission; the issuing bank will cover that amount. However, if you want out of the CD early, you could go back to your broker, and they could try to find someone to buy them from you. But in that case you would be the one paying the broker's commission.

Structured CD

The returns on a structured CD are tied to an index (such as the S&P 500), or they could be tied to currency movements or inflation. You are guaranteed not to lose money should the index decline, which is nice; but if it goes up, you'll only get to take advantage of a part of that gain. So if the S&P goes up 10 percent, you may only get 6 percent. While some of these are FDIC insured, the bank insures others. I recommend the FDIC-insured variety.

Ladder Your CDs

Basically, divide your CD money into four or five pots of money, then invest the portions into CDs that will come due over the next five years. That way, when interest rates rise (and they will), you won't have to wait five years to take advantage of the higher rate; you'll be able to roll over the CD that matures next. This strategy also gives you more access to cash should you need it.

A Final Note on Investing

Part of living the Sustainable Lifestyle Habit means taking care of first things first before you take the next step. Whether you are investing in household goods, appliances, short-term savings, CDs, or 401(k)s, it's important to remember that a healthy "bank" means that you are not ready to invest in the stock, bond, or real-estate market until you have met the following conditions:

Debt-Free. You've paid off consumer debt, including all credit cards.
Savings Full. There is an accessible savings account you have fully funded with at least six months of living expenses.
Retirement Too. Make sure you're funding your future before you invest in the market. Be sure you've funded some kind of retirement vehicle.

9.

De-Stress for Less

*Learn how to relax and enhance your
health without breaking your budget by
implementing these practical tips.*

Jennifer was a mom on the run. She worked part-time
building a home-based business and juggled the needs of three young children as well as her husband's, who had a demanding career as an army officer. Her days consisted of carpools, homework, household chores that never ended, work demands, and sometimes the added stress of having to deal with the single-mom routine while her husband was deployed. Jennifer could feel the stress starting to affect her body and mind. She often found herself short-tempered and out of sorts. Her best friend, Nancy, decided to help her de-stress. With the assistance of several friends, she treated Jennifer to a gift of a mom's day out at a spa. But it wasn't just any kind of spa; it was the Beverly Hilton—the luxury hotel that has catered to Hollywood stars since the 1950s and the home of the Golden Globes award show.

At first, Jennifer didn't want to accept the lavish gift, but then she discovered that her friends had purchased the package on Travelzoo.com. It was a spa package worth five hundred dollars and included valet parking (where she saw Ron Howard having his car parked), a one-hour relaxing massage, a heavenly one-hour facial, tea and scones, a facial masque (complete with cucumbers on her eyes and soothing music playing in her ears), and a fabulous finish to the day with a poolside meal (she could have sworn she saw Owen Wilson's twin sipping on iced tea). The package only cost her friends thirty dollars each (a total purchase price of $129). It was a day that renewed and refreshed Jennifer.

Wouldn't you like to have friends like Jennifer's? Whether you would or not, it's essential to your physical and mental health to take time to unwind, let go, relax, and play on a regular basis. We were designed with a mind that needs downtime, souls that need refreshment, and a body that needs sufficient, quality sleep within every twenty-four-hour cycle. While a certain amount of stress is healthy and motivates us toward productivity, too much persistent pressure takes the joy out of life and can literally kill us.

> Everything is under the power of choice, but once a choice is made, we become a servant to it.
>
> —Edwin Louis Cole

Hyper Speed, Hyper Stress

In our current high-tech culture, people expect immediate responses and solutions. As a result, we are constantly responding every minute to e-mail, text messages, and phone calls. We have become slaves to the very tools that are supposed to make our lives easier! In the process, we run out of time and energy on a regular basis. Our relationships are strained, our minds overstimulated, and our bodies neglected. This way of living is not healthy, nor is it normal. Most importantly, it is not necessary. Take a moment one day simply to sit quietly and observe people in a local coffee shop. You'll be amazed at how few are talking and looking each other in the eye without frequent interruptions from their phones or laptops. In the last couple of years, I have tried to take intentional blocks of time—especially in the evening or weekends—to avoid my phone for hours at a time. My family and close friends know my private home number and can call me in an emergency.

A life of balance requires sacrifice. We must invest in things that have long-term value over short-term gain. We are a lot like airplanes: we can only carry a limited amount of luggage. If we get overloaded, we may go down! Despite our best efforts, when we take on too much, we don't end up doing well at anything. In essence, to live in balance, we have to minimize our load. We can and do make time for that which is most important to us . . . right now.

The problem is that we pay a price for too often choosing now over later. No one will make you take a break from working a twelve-hour day to go for a walk. You won't get a fine for eating two doughnuts for breakfast every morning. No one will stop you from running up your credit card debt—at least until you hit your limit! But day after day there are consequences for our habitual choices. Stress that drains us of health, wealth, and happiness is one of those consequences.

Applying New Habits to De-Stress Your Life

If the choices you have made in the areas of work, money, or your body are starting to cost you more than you bargained for, then it is time to make some changes that will move you in a new, healthier direction.

The In and Out Habit reminds us that putting in too many stressful days without sufficient outlets for unwinding can rob us of joy and peace of mind, not to mention good health. While we may not have a spa day gifted to us next week, we can implement the 3D Habit and *determine* to schedule quiet moments (like a relaxing bath or walk in nature) into our lives, which can temporarily *distract* us from the work or other stresses that can consume every waking moment. Keep in mind, even God rested after six days of creating our magnificent world!

Even good things can become our enemies when taken to excess. A practical way to *distract* yourself from worry and too much focus on your to-do list is to incorporate the You Are What You Think Habit into this area of your life as well. If you live under constant stress, choose to repeat a few key self-talk phrases that will help you change your focus and responses to life. Here are a few practical statements that have worked well for me:

- *I choose to let go of things that are out of my control and focus on things that I can control, like my own thoughts and actions.*
- *I schedule downtime into my life and allow myself to set aside my busyness and deadlines for designated times of relaxation and renewal.*
- *I focus on the task at hand and refuse to worry about something I cannot deal with at the moment.*
- *I practice an attitude of gratefulness and joy, looking for the positive lesson whenever possible.*

In order to embrace fully the value of free time, we need to remind ourselves of the importance of recreation and relaxation in our overall quality of life and productivity. Our families, marriages, and friendships all need time to regenerate and celebrate so we can be refreshed and ready to face the next round of daily demands of modern living. Unfortunately, if we are not mindful, those rewarding activities can become costly and negatively impact our budgets—which puts us right back into stress mode!

WEALTH

66 Learn how to unwind physically and enhance your health without breaking your budget by implementing these practical tips. **99**

You can get the stress out of your life without breaking your budget if you follow a few steps to de-stress for less. Following are some creative ways to relax and be entertained while paying attention to your bottom line. I (Ellie) encourage you to pursue a sustainable lifestyle of balance, because the price we pay for living under constant stress is much too high. In fact, a CNN poll reveals that the number one reason for stress in most countries is money. The countries most stressed about money are Malaysia, China, Singapore, and the United States. The countries least stressed about money are Russia, France, and Italy.[1] It would be self-defeating to ask you to be less stressed about money and then suggest ways to de-stress that cost a lot of money. So this section will focus on ways to de-stress for less.

De-Stress for Less on the Run

As a mom of many children, I'm often a mom on the run. I've seen the price that people pay for never slowing down, and the cost can include frequent headaches, arthritis, high blood pressure, and even heart attacks. I determined when my children were young that I would learn to do things that relieved me of the pressures of a large and busy family. I also learned that some of the simplest activities could bring the most enjoyment. Here are some simple and free options I've used many times over the years to de-stress my life:

- Take a power nap.
- Listen to soothing music.
- Listen to an audiobook.
- People-watch on a bench.
- Talk to God.
- Light a candle.
- Eat a sack lunch at a park or somewhere outside.
- Take a stroll, and stop to smell some roses.

I know you are aware of these simple pleasures, but do you practice them? Intentional breaks from your usual routine can make a huge difference not only in your stress but also in your overall productivity later in the day.

De-Stress for Less When Going Out

If entertainment and eating out is scheduled into your spending plan, then there's no stress of going off budget. But what if you could go out twice as often and still stay on budget? Here are some ways to have twice the fun at the same price:

School Discount Cards. Help your favorite student by purchasing the school's discount card. Almost every school offers these as part of their fund-raising efforts. Most cards cost about ten dollars and are good at dozens of local businesses for savings on movies, spa services, haircuts, pizza, and more. We saved loads with a local coffee shop's "buy one, get one free" offer. My friends kept wondering why I chose the same location each time we met for java—because I saved $350 over the course of a year!

Entertainment Books. Entertainment.com offers a coupon book that costs between $25 and $45. Preview the coupon booklet for your area to be sure it includes savings at places you would normally go. You'll save on movie theaters, theme parks, sporting events, and local shops. The average advertised total book savings is $17,000. If you redeem 25 percent of the coupons, you would realize an annual savings of $4,250. Even a mere 10 percent redemption is a savings of $1,700 per year.

Facebook and Twitter. Follow local eateries and cafés to get real-time alerts on daily specials and freebies. For example, my college daughter, Bethany, follows her favorite cupcake shop on Twitter and gets a word of the day for a free treat.

Share and Save. Split a meal with your spouse or friend, and order an appetizer to share as well. Drink water instead of soda. You'll have a healthier wallet and waistline!

Local Newspaper. Check out your paper's Lifestyle section for "buy one, get one free" offers and special days for special deals.

Restaurant.com. Want to try a new restaurant but don't want to pay full price? Go to Restaurant.com, a site that issues printable gift certificates. Pay $10 to $15 for a $25 gift certificate. We usually buy these types of coupons on sale for only $3 and save even more. Go to Travelzoo.com or RetailMeNot.com to get the coupon codes for sales. The average restaurant bill for a family of four is $86. A weekly savings is $43 x 52 weeks or $2,236 annually.

De-Stress for Less on a Vacation

Since the recession, the idea of a "staycation" has become popular. A family camps out in the backyard or does something special to make their time at home feel more like time away. While these are great ideas to save money for people on a budget, I believe there are other ways to get away from home and have an affordable vacation away. For one thing, you can check your local deals at Groupon.com or LivingSocial.com to get some really fun values. I went indoor skydiving for only $35 (a $110 value), and it changed my entire perspective! The following are some ways to get away for less.

JUST SAY YES AND THEN SAY NO

One of my readers, Debby Sanford, and her husband, Steve, had been married twenty years and only taken two family vacations during that time. They would get a little bit ahead financially and then something would happen to crack their vacation savings—a job loss, unexpected medical bills, or auto repairs. Then they heard about a time-share presentation offered by Hilton Grand Vacations Club in Las Vegas. Since it was only a four-hour drive from their home, they said yes to take a tour of the facilities in exchange for an affordable time at a posh place.

The Sanfords stayed at the luxury resort hotel for only $50 per night and also received $100 in chips, which they immediately cashed in for spending money. Since the suites had cooking facilities, they were able to inexpensively cover most of their meals. They spent two hours on the tour and time-share presentation, and then said no to the purchase of the time-share. The total cost for this vacation was $85 in gas and $105 for food.

If you choose to pursue this idea, be sure you are able to say no to a time-share sales pitch and ask questions about the "introductory" offer: How many nights does the fee cover? Are children allowed? Can you use all the facilities for free: parking, pool, gym, and Internet? Steve and Debby were pleased with their holiday fun and said they would do it again.

SAY YES TO SOMEONE ELSE'S YES

Another option is to share another family's regular time-share. Some couples get several weeks on their ownership program each year and cannot always take the time off to enjoy it. The McDonald family considers this a tithe of their financial resources and offers their time-share to families in their community for the facility cost they are charged.

Most time-share owners pay an average of $250 for the week they are at the facility. If you cannot find a solo time-share, then consider sharing space with a family in your church, work, or community who is willing to split that fee and share the space. You could even offer to pay the entire fee, because $250 is still an inexpensive rate for a week's worth of fun at a nice resort.

TWO FOR THE PRICE OF ONE

If you have friends you like a lot and think your friendship can survive the test of a family vacation, then double up with that family and cut your bills in half. One of my readers, Carole Bowman, wrote me about her family's experience with the Healy family. They enjoyed it so much that they made it an every-other-year tradition. The normal price of a weeklong mountain cabin rental with three bedrooms was $900. "We made sure that we knew all the costs ahead of time and that there were no financial surprises," says Carole. Each family paid $450 and their own gas for a vacation that might not have been available to them otherwise. "We couldn't swing nearly $1,000 for the week on my salary, but we could afford half that amount, and we've truly enjoyed our time off," said Dwennon Healy.

You don't have to rent a cabin to double up with another family. There are many different kinds of rentals found on Vacation Rentals by Owner (vrbo.com). Suite hotels that offer extra rooms are also an option, such as the ones found at Kayak.com or Cheaphotels.com. For those who love the great outdoors, sharing campsite fees or RV rentals can split the price of a camping adventure. At RVRental.com we found rentals across the country that ranged from $117 per day to $385 per day. Depending on the owner of the RV, other charges to consider are hospitality kits, kitchen kits, and/or emergency road kits. Cleaning fees will apply if the RV is not returned in the condition in which it was rented.

YOUR HOME IS MY HOME AND VICE VERSA

Swapping homes is an idea that has been around a long time but is gaining popularity due to an ever-increasing number of web-based exchange services, such as Homelink.org, Intervac.org, and HomeExchange.com. Many swappers like the ease of listing their homes and entertaining offers from places they never considered visiting. The other advantage is that instead of leaving your own empty house as burglar-bait, you have the place occupied while you're away.

Most of these exchange services charge $30 to $110 per year. If the listed date for a specific location isn't within your desired time frame, you can e-mail one of the swappers from that destination and ask if they could be flexible with their dates. But is it safe to turn over your home to someone else? Home swappers and exchange services report remarkably few problems. Just make sure the service you use is fully vetted and insured against theft or vandalism.

This alternative is especially attractive to families with children, for whom hotel stays and lots of restaurant meals are expensive. One strategy is to swap with families who also have children, thereby adopting a kid-friendly home. Another added benefit is that the kids enjoy playing with all those new-to-them toys.

The primary expenses you will have for this type of vacation are the travel costs to the destination. For the best airfares, go to BookingBuddy .com, which will check all the online travel service prices (Orbitz.com, Expedia.com, and Travelocity.com). Most swappers prefer to begin with an exchange near home to get their feet wet before they swap with a family in Italy or Bora Bora. A family of four in New York, purchasing advanced-fare specially priced tickets at $229 each, could pay the $85 swap fee and visit Paris for only $991. It is recommended that you leave detailed instructions or a "user's manual" for your home. Also, it's essential to check with your insurance company to make sure the new family is covered should something unforeseeable occur.

VOLUNTEER YOUR WAY TO A CHEAPER VACATION

Steve and Debby Trigg discovered their favorite family vacation spot when they had an ample budget for family fun. They went to a Christian campground in Colorado and fell in love with the staff, landscape, and activities. They also caught the vision of how combining ministry with vacation could help teach their kids the concept of servant missions.

When Steve's hours were cut back at work, their vacation budget was reduced. They opted to go back to the campground as staff for a week. While their workload was increased, they still had plenty of family time with a ministry emphasis. Steve said, "We decided to volunteer to teach our children the benefits of servant missions and *not* for the benefit of a low-cost vacation—that is a serendipitous blessing."

Instead of paying a thousand dollars for the week (which is still a bargain for paid guests), they had a working vacation for free. Not all campgrounds offer this kind of a trade-off, but if your family enjoys this kind of environment, it would be worth your time to contact a local retreat center or campground. Go to ACAcamps.org for the American Camping Association or try Google to enter your state and "Christian campground" to find a location near you.

Not all vacation packages are faith-based; some are education-based as well. Family Hostel (HostelWorld.com) offers trips that match families with learning vacations around the world. Elderhostel offers those fifty-five and older up to ten thousand options starting at as little as $556 for a six-day photography workshop in Massachusetts.

WildernessVolunteers.org is a nonprofit organization created in 1997, which offers people of any age a chance to help and maintain national parks, forests, and wilderness areas across the United States. Everything from trail maintenance to vegetation projects may be on the agenda. Participants provide their own camping gear and share campsite chores. Most Wilderness Volunteer trips last about a week and cost around $219.

No matter what your vacation budget is, it's important to take time off from the real world to create and develop a meaningful time to foster friendship, marriage, and family. In years to come, you may not recall the price of the condominium or quality of the room service, but you will remember those forever memories with the people you love—because they are *priceless.*

HEALTH

❝ Learn how to physically unwind and enhance your health by implementing a few practical tips. **❞**

After thirteen years as a labor and delivery nurse, I (Danna) moved into the corporate world of high finance and high stress. At thirty-five years old, I transitioned from a consistently active, fit lifestyle to one that demanded sixty or more hours of work plus fairly frequent travel. My daily lament, "There's not enough time in the day," was expressed in frequent bursts of exasperation. My lifestyle was out of whack, and it was affecting my personal health, my family, and robbing me of joy. I needed to reevaluate my lifestyle as it was definitely not sustainable. I was out of balance in my In and Out Habit—putting in way more time on the job than the overall reward of compensation and accomplishment. I needed to find ways to de-stress and practice the 3D Habit so I could live more intentionally.

Stress Kills

We've all heard the cliché "Stress kills." It truly does diminish our health and sense of well-being in significant ways. Listed below are just a few of many dangerous outcomes that prolonged stress can produce in our bodies:

- The stress hormone cortisol not only causes abdominal fat to accumulate, but it also enlarges individual fat cells, leading to what researchers call "diseased" fat.[2]
- Stress is linked to the six leading causes of death: heart disease, cancer, lung ailments, accidents, liver cirrhosis, and suicide.[3]
- Chronic stress floods the brain with powerful hormones that are meant for short-term emergency situations. Chronic exposure can damage, shrink, and kill brain cells.[4]
- Chronic stress increases cytokines, which produce inflammation. Exposure to constant inflammation can damage arteries and other organs.[5]
- Stress can alter blood sugar levels, which can cause mood swings, fatigue, hyperglycemia, and metabolic syndrome, a major risk factor for heart attack and diabetes.[6]

Don't Worry; Be Happy

There are many intentional actions that can decrease stress and in turn increase health and well-being. For example, laughing lowers stress hormones (like cortisol, epinephrine, and adrenaline) and strengthens the immune system by releasing health-enhancing hormones. Choosing to see our challenges as opportunities rather than obstacles can actually change the way we feel about our circumstances. How we choose (and learn) to deal with life's tests will greatly determine how resilient we will be both physically and emotionally. If you struggle like I once did with feeling stressed out much of the time, go back to chapter 2 and spend some time exploring your self-talk in this area.

Your Misery Factor

We can create a whole lot of self-inflicted pain in our lives by how we choose to see our current life situation. There are certainly times when circumstances are out of our control, and they can seem overwhelming. My pastor once said, "The difference between reality and our expectations equals the level of our misery." If our expectations are grossly unrealistic, we will live lives of discontentment, and our misery factors will be chronically high. For example, if you are married to a quiet and mild-mannered introvert and constantly compare him to someone like George Clooney, your misery will be great! By learning to live with an attitude of gratitude and seeing the "glass" of your life half full rather than half empty, you can not only lower your misery factor but your blood pressure and stress as well.

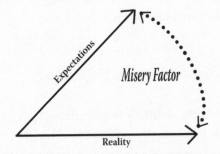

Stress is the trash of modern life—we all generate it, but if you don't dispose of it properly, it will pile up and overtake your life.

—Danzae Pace

Energize Your Body to Minimize Your Stress

No matter how much we want to simplify our lives, most of us are busy and need to find time-efficient ways to stay healthy. Just do the best you can, and do not get more stressed trying to add one more thing to your life. In this next section, I will show you how much of what we learned about the four health investment areas we discussed in chapter 8 (exercise, nutrition, sleep, and recreation/relaxation) can also help de-stress your mind and body!

STRESS BUSTER #1: EXERCISE

Even if you've been sedentary for years, a little movement can go a long way toward improving your health and ability to deal with stress. Here are seven reasons to get moving today.

Exercise

- improves mood and lightens depression by pumping out "feel good" hormones,
- alleviates anxiety and nervousness,
- releases muscular tension and stiffness,
- detoxifies your body by stimulating your lymphatic system,
- increases overall energy and mental alertness,
- promotes relaxation and well-being, and
- improves sleep patterns.

STRESS BUSTER #2: NUTRITION

The quality of our diet greatly impacts how we feel on a moment-to-moment basis. If you are sleeping adequately and getting regular exercise, but are still chronically fatigued, chances are your diet is to blame. Since nutrition was already addressed in detail in chapter 8, I simply want to remind you of three key nutritional issues that can influence your energy and sense of stress.

Start the Day Right

Eat a breakfast high in fiber and protein to stabilize your blood sugar and sustain your energy throughout the day. Try to eat at least 15 grams of protein and/or fiber total. Repeat this for any mid-morning snack and at lunch. By avoiding simple carbohydrates (bread, sugary cereals, and pastry) early in the day, you will start to notice a new verve of vitality—one that should promote the daily exercise you should be striving toward!

Hold Off on Empty Calories

As you learned in the last chapter, I am not a food purist. There is room for some "fun foods" in most of our diets if we keep it to a minimum. However, saving those empty calories until after lunch and perhaps even later will help you keep your energy high in the late afternoon when you start to wane.

Stay Hydrated

Every cell in your body needs high levels of water all day long to function properly. If there isn't enough water to go around, it is "borrowed" for the most essential systems. Nothing takes the place of pure, unadulterated water to hydrate, purify, and energize your body. If you wait until you are thirsty to drink water, you've waited too long. Many people live their lives subclinically dehydrated. Feelings of hunger, fatigue, and even headaches are often symptoms of dehydration. To maximize your energy, drink four to six ounces of water every waking hour—and more if you are exercising or in hot weather. The average person starts the day with tea or coffee; caffeine acts as a diuretic and actually diminishes hydration. Additionally, if you are having a challenge with stress, the extra stimulation of caffeine may not be helping you. Limit your caffein-ated drinks whenever possible.

STRESS BUSTER #3: SLEEP

Relax. Sleep. Things will be better in the morning, right? Not always. Many people suffer from insomnia and are wound so tightly that just *try-ing* to go to sleep increases their stress. Others are pushing themselves so hard at the job or with other life expectations, like exercise, they think they don't have time to sleep. It's been said, "We pay now or we pay later, but we always pay." That is the truth with choosing to skip sleep too often. If you are one of those people, do whatever you can to reverse this unhealthy pat-tern. Statistics reveal that those who don't get adequate sleep consistently age faster and tend to put on excess weight and keep it on.

Just to make it easy for you, here is a shorter recap of the tips I already shared in chapter 8 to help improve your sleep habit:

- Establish and maintain a regular time for going to bed.
- Design a winding-down plan the hour before bedtime.
- Turn off the television and mellow out.
- Practice deep breathing.
- Try melatonin.
- Carb up (moderately) to increase your serotonin "feel good" hormone.

STRESS BUSTER #4: GO BEYOND RELAXATION, AND HAVE SOME FUN!

One of the joys of my life is watching my two-year-old grandson, Demetre, play. He is an endless ball of all-boy energy. He laughs and runs and jumps and never stops having *fun*! As adults, we need to intentionally schedule moments in every day, hours in every week, and days in every month when we simply laugh, play, and celebrate life. In her wealth section, Ellie has given you lots of great tips for finding creative ways to do just that and not bust your budget. Now, it's your job to go out and have some fun!

When we manage our money and health issues well, we have more emotional margin in our lives to handle stress more effectively. As you consider the various health and wealth tips we've shared, we encourage you to put a few into practice. In closing, we'd like to share a broader perspective on the stresses of life for your consideration.

Questions to Lighten Your Load

Each day has stresses of its own. We know what it feels like to be constantly bombarded by dozens of choices every single day. Many of them will be good things. Often in areas of work or family, we feel guilty for saying no to those good things. Yet we know that there are only so many hours in a day. How can we choose the best from all the good? Perhaps these questions will help you in that process:

- Will this help me know and love my friends and family more?
- Will this help me grow in loving others more?
- Will this help me know and love God more?

In my most stressed-out years in the corporate world, I remember reading a quote that has been repeated endlessly over the decades but still resonates to this day: "No man ever said on his deathbed, 'I wish I had spent more time at the office.'"[7]

No matter where you spend the bulk of your day and energy, we all need to remind ourselves of what is most important. God did not create us as human "doings." We are human "beings"—created to experience life with Him and others through relationship. When we don't take time to stop and smell the roses or have quality face time with those we love, we burn out.

My favorite advice comes from the Author of life itself. Here's what He says: "Come away by yourselves to a secluded place and rest a while" (Mark 6:31).

10.

Raising Fit and Frugal Kids

*Help your children become physically and
financially mature adults by practicing key
habits you model and teach them to follow.*

If you're a parent, you want the best for your children.
You want them to be healthy, safe, and secure. You also want to instill values and habits that will help them develop lifestyles as they become young adults that enhance the quality of their lives and grow into responsible citizens. Between us (Ellie and Danna), we have raised eleven children. There were times when we wondered if they would ever embrace some of the health and wealth principles that we live by.

There was a time in my (Ellie's) early family life when we had three toddlers at the same time. If you ever want to observe the entitlement mentality in action, just watch children this age play together—if you can call it that. It's more like watching them fight together. Tiny tots have a skewed sense of reasoning. This mind-set was perfectly captured in this poem:

The Toddler's Creed
If I want it, it's mine.
If I give it to you and change my mind later, it's mine.

If I can take it away from you, it's mine.

If it's mine, it will never belong to anyone else, no matter what.

If we are building something together, all the pieces are mine.

If it looks like mine, it is mine.[1]

What's cute in a toddler is tedious in a teenager and downright debilitating in an adult. It's a sense of entitlement. Whether it's the food they want to eat or the things they want to buy, from spitting out their peas to begging for a sports car on their sixteenth birthday, children are wired to believe they are entitled to fulfill their immediate desires. It seems like one day they are toddlers demanding control of all the building blocks, and the next day they are young adults who feel entitled to all their parents' assets. They may think they deserve whatever they want, but it is our job to make sure they learn the principle of reaping what they sow by teaching them how to manage their own money and health in small ways from an early age.

Sadly, some children in the current millennial generation (fifteen- to thirty-three-year-olds) haven't grown up beyond their "terrible twos." As adults, their sense of entitlement is robbing them of their future. They are struggling to apply basic financial principles, especially when it comes to boundaries between their assets and their parents'. Sometimes they act as if "what's mine is mine, and what's yours is mine."

This applies to money matters, and it also applies to health. Children need to learn about money matters for themselves, but they also need to learn healthy habits, such as the In and Out Habit and that there are limits to what the body is capable of doing without proper rest, exercise, and nutrition.

Don't worry that children never listen to you; worry that they are always watching you.

—Robert Fulghum

There are three primary areas where people have fiscal and physical problems. If we can get a handle on these issues in our own lives and then teach our children to do the same, we can equip them for a brighter future. The three areas are

1. living an "immediate gratification" consumptive lifestyle,
2. accumulating debt or excess weight, and
3. failing to adhere to a budget or an eating plan.

On the other hand, if your kids grow into adults who can manage their health and wealth responsibly, they may

1. reach personal goals such as finishing college or staying physically fit,
2. live with less stress and have greater security, and
3. become responsible members of society.

WEALTH

66 Help your children become financially mature adults by practicing key habits you model and teach them to follow. **99**

My (Ellie's) kids are my calling cards—proof that it is possible to pass on healthy fiscal habits to our children. I am leery of financial experts who hand out parenting advice when they don't have kids or are not married. Wouldn't you rather get your advice from someone who has "been there, done that"? I would. That's why I look at the bottom line of those who are giving advice—how are their kids doing? Granted, not all kids take their parents' training to heart. As adults, they are free to make their own decisions, and we love them whether those decisions are good or bad. When it comes to money matters, we have always told our kids, "Our love for you is unconditional, but our money is conditional."

This means that if we said, "You shouldn't go to that college because it's twenty thousand dollars per semester and you'll owe too much in student loan debt" and then they did it anyway, we refused to cosign on the student loan. We continued to love that child as much as any of the others, but our money (or signature) was based on the premise that they make a good choice. We are not required to fund our kids' bad financial choices.

As I mentioned earlier, I have seven children, and two of them are by marriage. I call them my "children in love" because when I married my gorgeous guy, he already had two gorgeous girls. Consequently, I wasn't able to be the sole influence in their lives when it came to money matters. However, when it comes to the five kids who called me "Mom" 24/7, I have to accept responsibility for training them to become financially fit. Those kids are my calling cards because they are all set to graduate from college with no student loan debt, consumer debt, or car debt. They weren't perfect in their choices, and I wasn't a perfect parent. But overall, things fell in our favor because even if we failed in one area, we got back up and tried to do it right the next time. We learned from the In and Out Habit that if we sowed enough good information *into* them, then there could be a healthy harvest *out*. Thankfully, it's worked out that way in our young adult children.

Five Skills for Fiscal Success

I believe that children can grow up to be financially literate if parents model good habits as well as take time to teach and train them in the skills needed to realize fiscal success. The following five skills can be added at age-appropriate times in a child's life and modified with higher expectations and more complete training as they master the basics.

SKILL #1: THE ALLOWANCE LESSON

Some parents believe it's easier to give their kids money than it is to hassle with an allowance. I can see their point—administrating an allowance is hard work at times. But if we use an allowance as a teaching tool, then our kids can learn basic money management skills such as:

Budgets. Money has limits, and everyone needs to budget.

Discernment. There's nothing like having a child spend his own money to learn how to spend wisely.

Saving. Kids will want to spend less and save for items they desire.

Giving. Kids quickly learn how wonderful it feels to share with someone else.

Values. Kids tend to take better care of items they buy themselves.

Delayed Gratification. It takes a long time to save money and a little time to spend it.

The administration of an allowance is determined by the parent's guidance and the family budget. Here are some quick-start suggestions as you make allowance decisions:

Amount. This depends on the child's age and the family budget. For example, when our kids were young, we had a lot of kids but not a lot of money. Consequently, we paid fifty cents per age year per pay period to be paid every other week (you could make it every week if you desired). For example, a six-year-old would get three dollars every *other* week or three dollars every week, depending on the family's ability to pay. Our five children received allowance every other week because of our family size.

Consistency. Pay the same amount on the same day of the week or month. Just as you count on your paycheck, your children are counting on their allowances.

Responsibility. Establish each child's responsibilities. If they don't fulfill them, pay someone else to do the work. For example, I once paid our daughter Bethany fifty cents from our son Daniel's allowance to make his bed when he kept leaving the house without making it. He faced the penalty of losing part of his allowance and had the double whammy of watching his sister get his money. He never "forgot" again! This ties responsibility and allowance together.

SKILL #2: THE SAVING LESSON

Some kids are born savers (yours truly) and some are born spenders (my husband), and the Kays had a collection of both worldviews. No matter whether you are inclined to spend or save, parents can teach kids the secret of saving, which is a financial discipline that will serve them well for the rest of their lives.

> **Long-Term Savings Account Goals.** Establish an account where money will not be removed to cover short-term goals. This may be an account for a car, mission trip, college, or other big item.
>
> **Family 401(k).** Offer to match a quarter on the dollar for long-term savings.
>
> **Looney Tunes Accounts.** Many banks have fun kid accounts for younger children that can be opened with as little as five dollars and offer freebies as incentives to save.
>
> **Short-Term Goals.** Saving for a bike, doll, or video game also teaches delayed gratification.
>
> **Matching Funds.** Consider matching funds for the short-term goals if it will take more than a year for your child to save for the desired item.

SKILL #3: THE SHARING LESSON

One of the main reasons people have problems making ends meet is that they haven't learned the joy of giving. If you are tight with your money, then you tend to hold your funds with clenched fists rather than open hands. Your finances become stagnant, and you miss out on the freedom that comes with opening your heart (and your wallet) to others in need. This kind of giving is known as the tithe, because 10 percent (*tithe* means one-tenth) is the goal. But we have to start somewhere, and we can begin to teach our kids through simple actions.

Give. Teach them to give to nonprofit organizations or your church or synagogue, and let them observe your example.

Gather. Pull out groceries from your pantry and take them to a local food pantry.

Give Again. Collect outgrown clothing and toys to donate to a nonprofit thrift shop or homeless shelter.

Gain. By sponsoring a needy child, your child will gain perspective about how good we have it in the Western world. Sponsor a child from Compassion.com, WorldVision.org, or a similar organization, and post the child's photo on the refrigerator.

Give Some More. Bake and share goodies with their teachers, your neighbors, a postal worker, the local fire station, or a single-parent family.

SKILL #4: THE FUN BUDGET LESSON

When you make something fun, most children want to participate. What a great way to learn the In and Out Habit! We started making budgeting fun with our kids by creating fun kid budgets and establishing boundaries when we went out as a family. Keep in mind that in all the following categories, you are spending money in these areas anyway—it's your money. However, you can train your children as to how the money is allocated, and then it has the potential to become their money. Since these areas are budgeted, and since you are giving them a chance to come in under budget (and pocket the difference), it costs you nothing other than the time it takes to train them in this kind of money management.

Restaurant Fun. The next time you eat out, put your kids on a "budget" for their meal. Make it realistic with a little wiggle room. Have them budget for the entrée, drink, and dessert (you'll get the tip) and whatever they don't spend through their own choices (e.g., drinking water or foregoing a dessert) they get to keep, but they have to eat *something* and not just keep the money!

School Supplies. Figure the amount you would spend on these supplies per semester, and allow your child to spend from this budget and keep whatever is left over. It's amazing how few mechanical pencils they lose and how much better they take care of their backpacks!

Amusement Parks and Zoos. When you take a family outing to one of these places, set up a budget for each child that includes admission fees, food, drinks, and souvenirs. They will be surprised at how quickly the money goes, especially through the admission fees!

Clothing Budget. As your children become teens, the budget list expands and can include all kinds of other options, such as clothing. You decide what you'll budget on a semester's worth of attire, and whatever they don't spend, they get to keep. We tell our kids, "We'll pay for the item, and you pay for the brand name." For example, we pay $35 for a pair of tennis shoes, but if they want shoes that cost $80, they pay the $45 difference with their allowance money.

SKILL #5: A STRONG WORK ETHIC LESSON

I was talking to my husband over breakfast just this morning, and we were discussing an extended family member who never quite reached his potential. As we thought long and hard about what went wrong, I came to the conclusion, "He wasn't taught a work ethic. He was pampered and coddled. His parents always bailed him out of trouble, and he never really learned to work for the things that matter in life."

As parents, we can and should teach our kids a work ethic through jobs around the house and jobs outside the home as well. As long as you are willing to supervise your children's work, see to their safety when dealing with the public, and set boundaries that are appropriate for them, allowing kids to earn money outside the home can be a fun and worthwhile venture.

Here are some great ideas to help your kids raise their very own cash cow while enjoying the benefits of earning, saving, and sharing. For information on specific kinds of job descriptions, go to LeanBody-FatWallet .net for the downloadable jobs with descriptions, safety parameters, and suggested fees they should charge. The jobs you download at this site are written for a child reader with an adult supervisor in mind. The main thing is that as parents you need to be prepared to ensure that your child's job is safe and to maximize the teaching benefit of the work.

Parental Tips for Kids before They Start Working

When your child becomes employed, you are not necessarily their on-the-job-site supervisor. However, parental involvement is essential for a variety of reasons. For one thing, if your kid doesn't follow through with his work or if he does a lousy job, then it reflects poorly on your family and even you as parents. Safety is another concern—especially in today's culture. Here's a checklist for parents to review with their children before they accept a job.

SAFETY

Do you know the people your child is working for, and do you know their background? Will your child ever be in the employer's home? If your child is working for neighbors, and you prefer that your child work outside, then you need to give strict instructions that he or she is not to go into a stranger's home—even to go to the bathroom or get a drink. If you aren't familiar with that neighbor, then your child can come home to take care of the essentials. Or you might want to have him buddy up with a friend or sibling to do some of this work.

When it comes to jobs that require special equipment, be sure your child understands safety issues for a lawnmower, an edger, even pool cleaning equipment. If your child breaks someone's equipment due to improper use, then you (or your child) will need to pay for repairs. So be sure he or she knows how to operate the tools necessary for the job.

If your child ever feels uncomfortable on a job, then give him the freedom to come to you immediately with his concerns without fear of a scolding. It's far better to be safe than sorry when it comes to your child's well-being and the employer's property.

AGE-APPROPRIATE WORK

Parents, do you remember an incident in your life when you were given a task that was far beyond your ability? How did it make you feel? Were you frustrated or confused? Did you want to give up? Now, I'm *not* talking about the daily grind of parenting children or going through the "joys" of adolescence—I'm talking about the requirement to do a job that was not a good fit with your basic skills and abilities.

It's important that we try to match up our child with a job that is appropriate for her age. A seven-year-old shouldn't get a job walking a seventy-five-pound Saint Bernard—unless your seven-year-old is the size of an adult! There's a difference between childish irresponsibility and a child's ability. It's your role to help determine the difference in your child and her ability to adequately perform the task at hand.

A mismatched job will only lead to frustration and a bad feeling about work. On the other hand, there are some jobs that we don't think our kids can do, and they surprise us with their efficiency! The key is to supervise any of your child's work in which you're not sure of the age-appropriateness of the job. Once your children show you they can do it, let them excel!

ON-THE-JOB TRAINING

All the areas we've listed come with job descriptions and the details on how to do the job well at LeanBody-FatWallet.net. But there's no substitute for experience. Before your child ventures out on a job for pay, have him practice at home. In exchange for the training you give on how to do the job well, you will get the fringe benefits of a clean car, a weed-free flower bed, a freshly mowed lawn, sparkling windows, free babysitting, a clean garage—you get the idea, huh?

FOLLOW-THROUGH

Don't allow your children to do any job that you are not committed to helping them complete. Just as I ended up throwing a son's paper route on occasion (with the help of two small assistants), you will need to be prepared to babysit if your child gets sick at the last minute or find a substitute who is satisfactory to the employer.

If you have to finish a job due to your child's lack of responsibility or inappropriate behavior, then your child will pay you the *full* amount he receives for the job—even if he did half the work but didn't complete it. For example, when I had to throw Philip's paper route due to an after-school detention, he had to pay me twice the amount of a normal substitution. It's one of those tough-love lessons that will be priceless in the long run (even if it's painful in the here and now). In fact, Philip went on to have such a good work ethic that he earned his undergraduate and graduate degrees with no student loan debt.

QUALITY WORK

One of the boundaries you might want to establish before your child starts to work are the standards required for the job. Quality work and excellence should be the standard for our work as parents— and it's a good standard for our kids' work too! Part of this work quality will be demonstrated in the on-the-job training sessions, while another large part of it will only develop as your children work for other people.

It's important to praise your children when they do a good job. It's also wise to stress how one good job leads to another referral, which leads to more work, which will culminate in more income.

HEALTH

> 66 Children can become healthy and lean
> adults by practicing key habits that you
> model and teach them to follow. 99

There is a troubling and obvious trend manifesting all over America. You can see it every time you are out in a crowd—at the mall, an amusement park, or even church. It is visible, it is growing, and it is significant. The problem is the increasing number of not only overweight but also truly obese people. But the most troubling fact of all is that many, many of those people are children!

I (Danna) am very concerned as I watch more and more kids choosing television and video games over going out and riding bikes or actively playing. In my neighborhood, I see more youth on motorized scooters than ever. When our now-sixteen-year-old adopted grandson was younger, we implemented intentional timelines for watching television or playing video games so that he never developed a habit of sitting in front of a screen for endless hours. One year in junior high when his grades were not reflecting his ability, we acted on a previously set boundary and sold his Xbox game system. He was very unhappy, but two years later, he admitted the Xbox was a waste of time, and it had become too easy to "zone out" on mindless activity.

It's Not My Fault!

If you spend any time at all with eleven- to seventeen-year-olds, you will hear the words "It's not my fault" far too frequently. In recent years, there have been numerous criticisms and even threats of legal action against fast-food companies and other food-industry promoters of the American fat epidemic. But let's be completely honest and ask ourselves the right questions such as, "Are these companies telling us their products are healthy? Are they force-feeding us their supersized, calorie-dense products?" Of course they are not. We willingly line up, drive through, and dig into their burgers, side orders, and desserts with gusto.

The important question is this: Whose responsibility is it to choose the foods we eat and to live the lifestyles we live? Do we depend on American marketing to tell us what is good for us? That is absolutely absurd. That being said, our children are certainly not informed enough to discern wisely for themselves how they should eat and live for maximum health. That responsibility is up to parents, teachers, grandparents, aunts, uncles, and the like.

So what kind of mentor are you to the observers in your life? And I don't mean only children. Wives influence husbands and vice versa. Friends influence each other. And most importantly, parents are the key role models for their children. When Dad starts the day with coffee and a doughnut, what does that tell your son? And when Mom skips breakfast altogether, what example does she set for her adolescent daughter? The influence is great . . . the responsibility even greater.

If you don't want your son or daughter to be one of the increasing numbers of children who will have type 2 diabetes before they reach college, then you must take responsibility now. If that isn't a great incentive, I don't know what is!

Promote Healthful Changes

My wonderful, attractive, muscular, and loving husband, Lew, once was addicted to Diet Mountain Dew. It is full of caffeine, aspartame, and assorted other non-nutritive ingredients. Almost every day he'd grab a can of it and drink it on his way to work. The problem is that our son Jesse rode with him to school a couple of times each week. Despite Lew's overall appearance and general good health, his daily habit told Jesse that soda in the morning is okay. Oh really? Being the great guy that he is, Lew chose to modify his behavior (after a little gentle nagging from me). His highest motivation was Jesse—he could not deny that he was setting a bad example. Also, the facts about the chemicals passing his blood-brain barrier finally convinced him that his daily Diet Mountain Dew needed to become an occasional indulgence.

Once we realize that certain habits will eventually catch up with us in a negative way, how can we hide our heads in the sand without conviction? Hopefully we can't! We need to realize that our addictions to processed foods are wreaking havoc on our health. We may like the way it tastes, but does that justify taking it in at every whim? Few of us would ever consider taking heroin because of its dangerous side effects (and because it's illegal). But I suspect that more people will die this year from unhealthy eating and chronic obesity than they will from the dangers of heroin. Pretty scary, don't you think?

The point of my diatribe is not to make you feel guilty (but if guilt makes you take positive action, I'm okay with that). My point is to illustrate how reckless an unhealthy lifestyle can be in terms of its influence on others and on the quality of your life. If you don't care enough about yourself to make some much-needed changes in your habits, then care enough about those you love to be a mentor and model for them.

The truth of the matter is that women (wives, mothers, and friends) probably have more lifestyle influence on others than men do. Women still tend to be the key shoppers, cooks, and influencers in the areas of health and nutrition. But, guys, don't let my opinion stop you from making a difference. You don't have to beat your friends and family over the head with a "lifestyle stick" to nudge them toward healthy change. Gently encourage, model, and educate them to make their own health and habits a priority.

Find creative ways to get those you love into the act of living more healthfully. Promote more outings that are active. Get creative with preparing healthy foods in tasty ways that appeal to your children. By making healthful changes slowly, they may not even notice how much their meals and lifestyles have changed over time.

Growing Healthy Kids

Getting young children to eat healthfully is a huge challenge. The suggestions below will help parents and grandparents understand some important factors that influence young ones toward a lifestyle of healthy choices. Adults and children have their own unique responsibilities when it comes to mealtime. A child's responsibility is to chew and swallow. The parent's responsibility is to provide a variety of healthy foods in a relaxed environment. When these lines are crossed or confused, mealtimes can become very unpleasant.

It is important for parents to realize that every eating experience is an adventure for your child. There are many skills required for young children to master eating—from grasping a fork to capturing a roll-away pea, not to mention simply getting something slippery or scary-looking into their mouths and swallowing. Young children engage most of their senses (smell, touch, sight, and taste . . . sometimes even sound) when they are discovering and eating foods. They love to feel it squish or crunch in their little hands and often will play with it before it enters their mouths. Of course, we should accept that of our twelve- to twenty-four-month child. At six years old, food experiments at the dinner table are unacceptable.

Parents need to slow down and approach mealtime with the same wonder and amazement as the child experiences, realizing it takes at least eight exposures to a new food before a child can actually develop a positive taste for that food—no matter what his or her age. My son's sixteen-year-old girlfriend has had very limited exposure to the wide variety of foods our family eats. Sometimes I hear him prodding her on, saying, "Come on . . . try it . . . You'll like it!" I remind him that he hated avocados and artichokes until he'd experienced them many times—all the while smiling inside as I realize he's responded in healthy ways to our gentle, yet persistent encouragement to try new, healthy foods. Today he's on the varsity football team and is one of the strongest offensive and defensive linemen—thanks in part to healthy foods!

Taste Physiology

Your taste buds actually grow and mature as they are exposed to a variety of new tastes and textures. Unfortunately, most parents give up after one or two negative experiences, convinced that "Johnny just hates vegetables." But the truth is that Johnny never really got a chance to develop a taste for those veggies. Mom or Dad caved in to his initial negative response, and Johnny is ultimately the loser as his little body is short-changed by not receiving all the incredible nutrients God power-packed into many healthy foods.

There are four types of taste buds: sweet, sour, salty, and bitter. The sweet taste buds are strongest at birth and also surge in puberty, especially in girls. If we do not foster development of the other kinds of taste buds by introducing foods that promote their growth, our children will never learn to enjoy a wide variety of healthy foods. So how do we get our kids to even try foods that challenge their "sweet sensibilities"? Creativity, persistence, and patience are essential. The objective is to find something that will motivate your children to at least put the food in their mouths. Here are several ideas to help you in that quest:

CREATE "TASTE MOTIVATION" FOR YOUNG CHILDREN

If your child is into dinosaurs, then talk about foods such as asparagus or broccoli being "dinosaur" food. Tell them that one reason dinosaurs were so strong was because they ate lots of green foods. (Hopefully, they won't ask you if that's why they are extinct also!) Talk about how some foods build muscles (boys love that), make their hair shiny, or give them lots of energy to run faster and jump higher.

Give Them Tasty Condiments

You don't have to be a complete food purist. Realizing that your child's sweet taste buds are the most developed, you may want to add a slightly sweetened dip for fruits and veggies that are still not on your child's "favorite" list. Some kids simply want a flavor they recognize, such as butter or chicken broth, in some foods. Most active children can handle the few extra calories that help them enjoy the foods they need most but are resistant to trying.

Dealing with the Veggie Rejecter

You may have a child who clenches his teeth and begins a forceful standoff anytime veggies are even mentioned. Take heart. There are five fruits that provide very similar nutritional value to many key veggies. They include kiwis, mangos, cantaloupe, strawberries, and apricots. You can also sneak carrot juice and "super green" supplements into fruit smoothies or protein shakes, and they won't even know it. Don't ever stop offering veggies to your kids. Research shows that children who are introduced to vegetables early in life will return to them in their teens and adulthood.

The Top Five Nutritional Roadblocks for Young Children

Before you get too concerned about fine-tuning your child's diet, be sure you are addressing the top five nutritional roadblocks for young children.

ROADBLOCK #1: TOO MUCH JUICE

Train your children from an early age to quench thirst with water. When juice is given, dilute it with water and limit it to six ounces per day. Rather than juice, whole fruits will provide fiber that slows the release of fruit sugar into the bloodstream.

ROADBLOCK #2: TOO MANY HYDROGENATED FATS

Hydrogenated fats, found in most margarine and processed foods, are known to limit nerve transmission and ultimately lead to cardio-vascular disease. Pay attention to how many foods your family regularly eats that come in bags and boxes, because that is where you will find most of your troublesome foods. Try to increase both snack and mealtime foods that are found in the perimeter of your grocery store in the produce, dairy, and meat/poultry/fish sections. These are the foods that are closest to the way God made them originally!

ROADBLOCK #3: TOO MUCH SUGAR AND SODA

Children are naturally drawn to sweet tastes, so we need to be selective and wise as to just how much sugar they are ingesting. As noted above, using sweet flavors creatively and in combination with healthy foods is ideal. Too many parents think it is normal to provide candy, cookies, or treats to their children every day. If that is your habit, it will be theirs as well. We all enjoy a little sweet indulgence, and if kept to very small amounts, most children and adults don't suffer negative results. But if dessert or candy is a daily part of your routine, it may grow into a bigger problem for your child later. In addition to being very high in sugar, soda is also high in phosphoric acid (bad for the bones) as well as tin and aluminum. However, offering your child diet sodas as an alternative is even scarier since noncaloric sweeteners such as NutraSweet have been shown to potentially cross the delicate blood-brain barrier and possibly impact cognitive function.[2] Consider one soda a week as a healthy compromise for older children who are likely to be exposed to sugary drinks sometimes on a daily basis. Most people don't realize that a moderate sugary treat can actually diminish immunity (by impacting white blood cell production) for several hours after ingestion.

ROADBLOCK #4: TOO LITTLE FIBER

Read the labels on your bread, cereal, and cracker packages. Look for good sources of fiber with listings of whole grains and minimal preservatives. For bread, try to find two to four grams of fiber per slice. For cereals, aim for four to six grams per serving. On the subject of cereal: do not cave in! Most children's cereals are so low in fiber and high in sugar that it is like starting your child's day with a bag of M&Ms. Buy one favorite sugary, sweet cereal and let your child have a small bowl once a week as *dessert*!

ROADBLOCK #5: TOO LITTLE PROTEIN EARLY IN THE DAY

Good sources of protein at breakfast and lunch are essential for high energy and diminished sweet cravings (this goes for you also, parents). Eggs, protein shakes, and peanut butter on whole wheat toast are all great sources of protein that will get the whole family off to a healthy start. The protein you plan for dinner is less important than what you serve for breakfast and lunch. Get creative and find fun and healthy ways to increase protein early in the day. Nuts, string cheese, and chicken strips are great choices.

Taking Responsibility with Grace

It is essential that as parents we realize we are laying health and wealth foundations for our children that will impact them for a lifetime. If we get lazy and follow the path of least resistance by caving in every time they ask us to buy something or letting them eat unhealthy treats, they will inherit poor attitudes and habits that will impact their physical and financial wellness for decades. On the other hand, we don't have to be overly legalistic either. Find the balance between excellent choices and intentional indulgences that celebrate a sustainable lifestyle your children can live with long term.

Incorporate all the new habits you are learning with raising your children. How do you model the 3D Habit so they learn how to wisely *determine* the choices they make when they are tempted? Pay attention to how you *delay* and *distract* yourself from unplanned indulgences and how you help them do the same. Discuss the In and Out Habit at an age-appropriate level when it comes to their allowances or the foods they choose to eat. By teaching and practicing the four habits of this book with your children, you will reinforce them in your own life as well.

Healthy Messages to Grow Healthy Kids

What words do you use that influence how your kids think about food, money, and living a healthy and responsible lifestyle? Words have great power. Most of us can easily recite some of the negative messages we heard over and over as a child that haunt us for a lifetime if we don't learn and practice techniques to erase and replace those statements. Many adults lament being told things like, "You'll never amount to anything," "You aren't smart enough to go to college," "You are lazy," "You are messy," and "You are unreliable." As we've already learned, we believe what we are told and what we tell ourselves most often. So the words you choose to use with your children (in every area of their lives) matter.

As you determine to help your children grow healthy habits, choose to become mindful of the way you speak about spending, saving, eating, and exercise. By intentionally choosing specific statements that build up your child's positive attitude, you can use the You Are What You Think Habit to instill strong messages that can serve them well for a lifetime. Here are a few examples of strong, positive self-talk messages you may want to try at home:

- *We are a family that plans ahead and chooses where we will spend our money intentionally so we can meet our bigger goals, such as vacations, college funds, and a better home for everyone to enjoy.*
- *Your allowance allows you to practice three uses of money that are all important: saving, giving, and spending.*
- *We choose to eat healthy foods that help us grow strong because our bodies work best when they are given the best fuel possible.*
- *We eat "fun foods" in small amounts because too much makes us feel tired and is bad for our bodies.*

Giving for Wealth and Health

Give from the storehouse of your time, talent,
or resources to meet someone else's need.

One Saturday afternoon, a busy mom named Cindy was tooling down Main Street with four bags of groceries in the trunk of her car. She had recently begun to learn the strategy of "extreme couponing" and had only paid ten dollars for all her loot. When she stopped for a lady walking in the crosswalk, she noticed the woman was blind and was being helped by her four young children. One of them was pushing a metal cart with one small bag of groceries. Cindy assumed they had come from the nearby supermarket. Then something strange happened.

A still, small voice spoke to her heart and said, *Stop your car and give them your groceries.* Cindy was blown away. She'd *never* had any idea like this before and quickly tried to put it out of her head. But she couldn't shake the thought, which kept repeating in her mind. She was a little disturbed by the situation. *It must have been the pizza I had for lunch,* she decided.

Again, the impression came to her, and this time it was crystal clear. *Give them all your groceries. It's your blessing to choose or refuse.* She realized that it wasn't a creepy thought she was having; it was a divine thought—a directive to reach out in kindness to a stranger—a God-sized idea. Cindy immediately turned her car around, found the young family, and ran to them with the groceries in her arms. As she placed the bags in the lady's metal cart she said, "I know you don't know me, and that's not important. What is important is that you know that God loves you and I want you to have these groceries."

The woman was bewildered and overcome by the kindness of a stranger who was meeting her obvious need. It was hard for her to grasp the idea that God had sent someone to meet her on the side of the road with her four children in tow. The blind woman stood on the sidewalk and didn't seem to know what to do. She began to cry. Softly she exclaimed, "Thank you! Oh, thank you!"

Even though the mother of four didn't know what to do about the groceries and the kindness of a stranger, the kids knew what to do— they immediately started going through the bags. "Hey, Mom! There's cereal!" shouted her nine-year-old son.

"There's milk too," exclaimed the slightly younger daughter. "We can have milk with our cereal!"

Then the two-year-old happily said something you never want to hear from a two-year-old, "Mama, there's eben *gum!*"

There's a lesson to be learned from this true-life story. In the store earlier, Cindy was practicing new methods of stretching her family's food budget. She was being wise and resourceful with her food budget. At the time, she had no way of knowing that she was about to become God's provision for another mom in need, to provide not only some of her financial needs but her physical and emotional needs as well. Sometimes we are wealthy in order to help others become healthy. Conversely, we are sometimes healthy so that we can physically be a provision for others in need. It's important to give through our health and our wealth.

Everyone can give and become a provision to others in need by looking for ways to share their health and wealth in selfless ways. By giving to others we become more balanced emotionally and experience that feel-good high that comes when we make someone else's life a little brighter. When you practice sharing from the storehouse of your time, talent, or resources regularly, you can actually get hooked on giving—a truly healthy addiction.

No one is useless in this world who lightens the burdens of another.
—Charles Dickens

WEALTH

66 Give something from the storehouse of your time, talent, or resources to meet someone else's need. 99

There are endless ways to give of your finances within your local community and even across the globe. In the Kay family, we make our local church our first priority. We have found that our church is able to invest in our community in ways that match our vision for giving. If you are a member or regular attender of a church, it makes sense both spiritually and practically to support the church where you worship and are personally blessed. Of course, in addition to your financial support, you can also give of your time, talent, and energy. As Christians, both our families believe in the biblical principle of tithing—giving 10 percent of our income to God's work—as a first priority. We believe this is not under compulsion or some kind of legalistic rule but rather given freely out of love for God.

Give to Charitable Organizations

In addition to supporting your local church, consider giving clothing, time, furniture, and other goods and services to organizations that have a positive impact both in your area and beyond. Following is a list of some places where you can give. I'm sure you can think of many more. Please be sure to send us your ideas via our contact page at www.LeanBody-FatWallet.net. We are always encouraged by the new and creative ways that our readers make the world a better place.

HOMELESS SHELTERS

The volunteers who work at homeless shelters are truly on the front lines of fighting hunger. These organizations welcome not only your food and clothing donations but your time as well. There's nothing like a day serving soup to make a family thankful for the food they eat each day in their own homes. Our family tries to help homeless people when we see them on the street holding a sign that says, "Will work for food." While we don't feel comfortable giving money that could possibly go to support addictive behavior (some "professional" homeless folks make up to fifty dollars an hour), we still want to do *something*.

At age nine, our son Daniel came up with the idea of keeping non-perishable foods in the console of the Suburban. When we saw someone in need on the street, we handed them cans of chili or pasta meals. When we started doing this, the children were so eager to give to the homeless that they tried to find them on the street. They often decided someone was homeless whether they were or not.

"There's a homeless man!" shouted Jonathan one day as he pointed to a man by the side of the road. I looked where Jonathan was pointing and saw a young man on a bicycle. I slowed down the car. "Jonathan, that is not a homeless man. He's on a bicycle and his blue jeans are just dirty—he doesn't even have a sign!" Disappointed, Jonathan shrugged. "Well, he looked kind of lost to me. Maybe we could give him some clothes soap." It's the heart that counts.

CRISIS PREGNANCY CENTERS

These centers provide tangible help to pregnant women by providing maternity clothes, toiletries, diapers, formula, baby food, and groceries. Look up your nearest crisis pregnancy center online. They need hands to help and resources to give these needy women. Our daughter Bethany asked us to save the shampoo, conditioner, and lotion bottles from our hotel stays and then she collected them to donate to these shelters.

OPERATION GRATITUDE

Go to OperationGratitude.com to see how you can help put together a care package for a military member stationed overseas. These packages may be the only mail that some military members receive if they have no family support at home. There are distribution centers where you and your family can put together packages that include comfort items from home that tell these service members you appreciate what they do and are proud of them. This year, our son Joshua helped us assemble these care packages and enjoyed doing something helpful for others.

WOMEN'S SHELTERS

Women and children who seek these shelters often come for help with only the clothes on their backs. These shelters especially need trial-size toiletries, as their occupants may stay for anywhere from a day to a year. Don't be surprised if you are asked to drop off the needed items at an office downtown rather than the shelter itself—confidentiality is often necessary for the protection of the women and children.

One year, during a six-month period, I obtained thirty-five bottles of hair coloring free with my couponing. I donated them to a shelter with support from the local grocery store with the understanding that the women could exchange them for the right shade. Sometimes it's the little things that make the difference in a difficult situation.

POSTAL WORKERS' FOOD DRIVES

Every year postal workers collect millions of pounds of nonperishable foods for people in need. In addition, there are Boy Scout/Girl Scout food drives throughout the community. You can even work with your employer and set up a food-drive box in your workplace or school.

You can engage your children or kids from a local school by helping you deliver food to a local food pantry.

THE SALVATION ARMY, GOODWILL INDUSTRIES, AND VETERANS

These nonprofit groups help support disabled Americans through the provision of jobs. Be sure to drop off your donations during business hours so you can secure a tax-deductible receipt. They also help provide clothing to third-world organizations. It's wonderful to think that your castoffs could be clothing kids half a world away.

> We make a living by what we get. We make a life by what we give.
>
> —Winston Churchill

Twenty Gifts You Can Freely Give

No matter what your financial standing, there are many gifts of tremendous, even eternal value that can be given at no cost to you at any time and in any place:

1. Fix broken fences by mending a quarrel.
2. Seek out a friend you haven't seen in a while or who has been forgotten.
3. Hug someone you love, and whisper, "I love you so."
4. Forgive an enemy, and pray for him.
5. Be patient with an angry person.
6. Express gratitude to someone in your world.
7. Make a child smile.
8. Find the time to keep a promise.
9. Make or bake something for someone else—anonymously.
10. Speak kindly to a stranger.
11. Enter into another's sorrows with empathy and an open ear.

12. Smile. Laugh a little. Laugh a lot.
13. Take a walk with a friend.
14. Send a lonely person a handwritten note.
15. Lessen your expectation of others.
16. Apologize if you were wrong.
17. Turn off the television and talk.
18. Pray for someone who helped you when you hurt.
19. Give a soft answer even though you feel strongly.
20. Make friends with someone with whom you have nothing in common.

HEALTH

❝ You can give something from the storehouse of your time, talent, or resources to meet someone else's need. **❞**

When we think about giving, most of us think first about our money or other material resources. But one of the most generous gifts is that of our time. As I (Donna) watch my children grow into adulthood and my adopted grandson go from a teenager to a young man, I realize that one of the best gifts I can give is that of staying healthy. It's been one of my greatest joys to become best friends with my two grown daughters. I am the first person they call (after their husbands) when something great happens or when facing a difficult situation. We relish our Sunday family days when we all sit for hours around the dinner table laughing and sharing. I ski with my eighty-five-year-old father; and my husband, Lew, scuba dives with our son. Staying fit and healthy allows us to fully engage in life with those we love. It also helps minimize the risk (though never fully guarantee) that we will become a burden to our children later in life.

By choosing a healthy lifestyle and modeling it to others, you can invest your time, energy, and efforts into others' lives. From your family to your community and even across the globe, staying healthy can allow you to roll up your sleeves and meet others' physical needs personally.

World Vision—Give the Gift of Health to Children across the Globe

In the years that I struggled with bulimia, I sometimes felt like I was eating enough to feed a third-world country. Ironically, in the last decade I have partnered with an amazing organization that makes it their purpose to make sure children across the globe have the food, clean water, medicine, and other essentials necessary to live. Founded in 1950, World Vision has been changing lives for over sixty years.

According to UNICEF, approximately seven million children die every year from preventable causes.[1] We would never stand for this in our own community or state. Sadly, pain and suffering that is out of sight is often out of mind as well. You cannot personally alleviate world hunger, but you can change the lives of one or two children at a personal financial cost of about a dollar per day—a single dollar can significantly change a life. I have often said that the six dollars my family spends each day on the six children we sponsor is the most important financial decision we make. Not only that, we give the gift of encouragement and love by sending occasional notes and pictures to our sponsored children. A few years ago, my son Jesse (then age thirteen) was allowed to accompany me on a trip to Nicaragua with World Vision. We met two of our own sponsored children as well as my daughter Jill's sponsored child. Jesse was greatly impacted by the poverty in this area of the world. Just as important, he was forever touched by the level of gratitude the children displayed for the simplest of gifts like a soccer ball or coloring book. If you have never considered giving in this way, try it. The return on investment to your own heart is beyond worldly value.

Pay It Forward—Share Wealth and Health with Others Daily

Be on the lookout for ways to give the gift of health and wealth regularly in your community. As Ellie shared at the beginning of this chapter, we are often used as conduits of blessing to others who have less. Whether the lack is in material things or even knowledge, we can find creative ways to pay it forward.

You may want to help a young wife or mother learn how to feed her family more nourishing foods by offering to share healthy recipes or tips on how you get your children to eat veggies. Encouraging a friend who is battling with her weight can be as simple as taking walks and sharing some of the new habits you have learned in this book. By cultivating a giving heart and a willingness to share all that you possess—time, talents, and possessions—you will discover endless opportunities to invest in others.

It's not how much we give but how much love we put into giving.
—Mother Teresa

12.

Realizing Your Lean Body and Fat Wallet

Create and follow a simple action plan to reach your goals by focusing on a few key action items each day.

Now is the time to take action! As you take intentional, small steps in the direction of your goals, your life can begin to change in powerful ways. You have the knowledge to build some foundational habits so that you are no longer surviving by sheer self-discipline, but rather by new foundational habits that will support you internally and naturally.

Years ago, Dale Carnegie, after writing his now-classic book *How to Win Friends and Influence People*, made a wise suggestion to help his readers implement all they'd learned. He recommended that they go back one chapter at a time and practice what they learned from it. That is essentially what we hope you will do with this book. This last chapter is a practical one and will hopefully help you do just that. We've provided a brief recap and charts of the content from each chapter to jog your memory about all the things you've learned. You can use it as a menu to choose from as you create an action plan.

Writing down your daily goals and the action steps needed to move forward is an effective way to implement new health and wealth habits. Take some time to reflect on the items in the chapter recap and charts, and decide which habits, principles, and tips will most effectively help you design a sustainable lifestyle.

We've included a simple weekly worksheet to write down your goals and action plan. There is one for your health goals and one for your wealth goals. These are both available as downloadable PDFs on www.LeanBody-FatWallet.net. Every day of the week is listed so you can take notes as you follow through on the specific actions and check them off the list. We've created a sample to give you some ideas.

Don't try to take on too much at once. Determine one significant goal per area (health and wealth), and then choose the habits and practical tips that help you move forward. Repeat these action items daily for a full week and then fill out another form for the following week. As you create a new one each week, you can make modifications as needed to your plan.

Remember that it takes twenty-one days of repeated activity to even begin to form a new habit, so you will want to continue with certain actions until the habit takes root. One way you will know that a new habit is becoming strong and is your new autopilot is when you do not need to spend a lot of conscious effort or willpower to take action. The more you work on your new self-talk and practice new activities that support it, the faster those internal changes will occur.

Studies show that we reach our goals better with support. Consider inviting others to join you on your Lean Body, Fat Wallet quest. Accountability, encouragement, and community are wonderful motivators to follow through on the new you.

Use the following logs by checking off the new habits you are implementing each day.

My Lean Body Goal: Lose 15 pounds in 4 months

Daily Actions	Monday	Tuesday	Wednesday	Thursday	Friday	Saturday	Sunday
Habit #1—You Think Practice positive self-talk every time I look in the mirror and counter any lies with truth.							
Habit #2—3D *Determine* to stop eating sweets, *distract* myself with a healthy food option, and *delay* the impulse by taking a quick walk around the block.							
Habit #3—In and Out Use my phone app to track calories and walk three miles five times a week.							
Habit #4—Sustainable Choose a weekly food menu that I can live with daily, and prepare that menu for the week.							

My Fat Wallet Goal: Pay off our $1,000 Visa card in 6 months

Daily Actions	Monday	Tuesday	Wednesday	Thursday	Friday	Saturday	Sunday
Habit #1—You Think Remind myself that I can become debt-free and it is worth the effort.							
Habit #2—3D *Determine* to stop using the credit card, *distract* myself by leaving the credit card at home, and *delay* any online purchases for twenty-four hours to avoid impulse buys.							
Habit #3—In and Out Cut back on household expenses by shopping savvy and making phone calls to reduce costs, then take the saved money and put it toward the credit card.							

Habit #4— Sustainable Make sure I have a budget that will (1) save money and (2) be a budget we can live on for months at a time.							

My Lean Body Goal

Daily Actions	Monday	Tuesday	Wednesday	Thursday	Friday	Saturday	Sunday
Habit #1							
Habit #2							
Habit #3							
Habit #4							

Lean Body—Fat Wallet Total Recap Menu

My Fat Wallet Goal

Daily Actions	Monday	Tuesday	Wednesday	Thursday	Friday	Saturday	Sunday
Habit #1							
Habit #2							
Habit #3							
Habit #4							

Lean Body, Fat Wallet:
Total Recap Menu

Chapter 1: Habits for Health and Wealth

HOW DO YOU CHANGE A HABIT?
- In the human brain, the most dominant thought wins.
- We operate most frequently on the "autopilot" of our habits.
- You can change your thoughts that drive your emotions and habits.

THE FOUR LEAN BODY, FAT WALLET HABITS
1. The You Are What You Think Habit
2. The 3D Habit
3. The In and Out Habit
4. The Sustainable Lifestyle Habit

TOP TEN FAILURE FACTORS
1. Set unrealistic goals
2. Driven by the wrong motives
3. Believe failure is inevitable
4. Fulfill the need for immediate gratification too often
5. Influenced unduly by other people
6. Practice an all-or-nothing mentality
7. Rationalize and make excuses rather than taking responsibility

8. Displace emotional issues through overspending and overeating
9. Procrastinate rather than taking action
10. Lack the tools to make compounding incremental change

Chapter 2: The You Are What You Think Habit

THE YOU ARE WHAT YOU THINK HABIT
- This is the most foundational habit.
- It takes twenty-one days to begin to change our thoughts.
- Neuron pathways change in response to repetition.
- Practice makes permanent.

SIMPLE STEPS TO CHANGE YOUR MIND
1. Identify the lies you believe.
2. Take your negative thoughts captive.
3. Construct new thoughts to counteract the lies.
4. Repeat your healthy self-talk until new dominant thoughts form.

MORE STRATEGIES TO RENEW YOUR MIND
- Keep a thought notebook.
- Record your emotions and your thoughts.
- Use triggering events.
- Listen to healthy self-talk CDs.

Chapter 3: The 3D Habit

THE 3D HABIT
1. Determine
2. Distract
3. Delay

THE 3D HABIT IN ACTION
- This habit is your temptation deterrent strategy.
- Use it to deal with shopping urges.
- Use it to deal with eating urges.
- It works most effectively when you plan ahead.
- Use it in combination with healthy self-talk.

Chapter 4: The In and Out Habit

THE IN AND OUT HABIT
- It determines your bottom line physically and financially.
- To lose weight: put less food in—burn more calories (out).
- To lose debt and save: put less money out on purchases—put more into savings.
- Small stuff adds up.
- The four-cracker factor leads to weight gain.
- Five dollars a day keeps the sports car away.

IN AND OUT STATEMENTS TO CONSIDER
- I know exactly how much I eat/spend each day.
- I read labels for calories and price when I buy food.
- I maintain a very active lifestyle.
- I maintain a money budget.
- I exercise four or more days every week.
- I save money every month.
- I generally eat only when I'm hungry.
- I only buy things I plan to buy.

Chapter 5: The Sustainable Lifestyle Habit

THE SUSTAINABLE LIFESTYLE HABIT
- A healthy and sustainable lifestyle is one you can do most days for the rest of your life and still actually enjoy your life.

ASK YOURSELF
- Can I live this way most days and not feel totally deprived?
- Can I lead a fairly normal life with this particular approach?
- Will I be able to maintain this, or will I burn out?
- Do I have enough time to invest in this lifestyle most days for the rest of my life?

THE POWER OF INCREMENTAL CHANGE
- Incremental change compounds greatly over time.
- Small changes should not be underestimated.
- Incremental change can profoundly change your life.
- Pay attention to the small choices you make.
- Intentionally add positive small steps that move you in the right direction.

DESIGN YOUR SUSTAINABLE LIFESTYLE
WITH FIVE IMPORTANT STEPS
Step #1: Decide What You Want
Step #2: Decide Where to Start
Step #3: Decide What Distracts
Step #4: Decide How to Overcome Obstacles
Step #5: Decide When to Celebrate

Chapter 6: Balanced Bodies and Budgets

WEALTH

Ellie's Budget Plan Recap
- Establish current spending levels.
- Subtract current spending from income to get current budget expenses.
- Crunch the numbers on current spending levels with suggested budget percentages (or goal budget) to establish current financial status (either overspending or underspending in specific categories).

- Establish and commit to a new goal budget based on your family's unique situation and your desired financial goals.
- Commit to making spending/saving adjustments that will help you reach your financial goals and stick to the new goal budget.

Ellie's Budget Busters Recap

- Debt
- Impulse buying
- Comfort spending
- Gifts
- Vacations

HEALTH

Calories In Versus Calories Out

- Your body is a calorie-burning and -storing machine.
- Calories are the bottom line.

Resting Metabolic Rate (RMR)

- Never eat less than your RMR.
- Support a healthy metabolism by doing muscle work regularly.
- Support a healthy metabolism with frequent aerobic exercise.

Fat-Burning Facts

- The average woman burns about 1,700 calories per day.
- One pound equals 3,500 calories.
- Burn 500 excess calories per day to burn off one pound of fat per week.
- Burn 250 calories more, and eat 250 calories less.

Danna's Five Best Strategies for Consuming Fewer Calories

1. Use portion control.
2. Eat 30 to 50 percent less the last four hours of your day.
3. Fuel and burn all day long.

4. Cut out all processed foods, white flour, and sugar.

5. Apply the ultimate strategy: go to "calorie college."

Danna's Six Best Strategies for Burning More Calories

1. Do the exercise and activities you like best.
2. Engage exercise at the time of day that works best for you.
3. Include healthy self-talk to overcome a "couch potato" mind-set.
4. Consider daily exercise your ultimate goal.
5. Use an accurate activity monitor for a reality check and motivation to move more.
6. Find creative ways to get longer and higher-burning aerobic workouts.

Danna's Triple-Burn Exercise Tip

- Walk on the treadmill at 12 percent grade for one hour daily!

Chapter 7: Fat Cells and Fat Sales

WEALTH

A Motivating Reality Check

- Evaluate your own debt story.
- Understand the high cost of debt.
- Apply unexpected income toward your debt load.
- Apply the Lean Body, Fat Wallet Habits to saving money and getting out of debt.

Save Money in the Grocery Store by Layering the Savings

- Understand important couponing strategies.
- Use coupon apps and websites.
- Clip every coupon, share the savings, and start a "swapbox."
- Use price matching.
- Search high and low for bargains.

- Use a shopping list—don't leave home without it!
- Hungry? Eat first, or stay at home!
- Only buy items that are on sale, and stock up.

Save Money Online by Layering the Savings
- Shopping robots
- Coupon codes
- Online rebates

Save Money When Buying a Car
- Drive the paid-for car you have longer, and start a car fund.
- Negotiate the car price separately from a trade or financing.
- Negotiate the trade-in after you've negotiated the car price.
- Negotiate the financing separately, and try to secure your own first.

HEALTH

The You Are What You Think Habit
- Healthy self-talk is essential for overcoming emotional eating.

Personal Temptation Exercise
- The temptations I most want to overcome are:
- The lies I believe related to these temptations are:
- The new messages I will use to replace these lies are:
- My positive power layer is:

Temptation and the 3D Habit
- This habit is your strategy for intentionally addressing your weaknesses.
- Make temptation more difficult (move the cookies; hide the remote).

Four Key Concepts to Overcome Emotional Eating
1. Legalize food
2. Manage your hunger scale

3. Identify your eating triggers
4. Keep a food journal

Chapter 8: Healthy Investments for Body and Bank

HEALTH

Your Body—Your Vehicle for Life
- You can't trade in your body, so take good care of it.

The 70/30 Rule
- You have control over your lifestyle.

Essential Health Investments
- Exercise
- Nutrition
- Sleep
- Recreation and relaxation

Health Investment #1: Exercise
- Controls weight
- Improves mood
- Boosts energy
- Promotes better sleep
- Improves your sex life
- Relaxes and reenergizes
- Lowers disease risk
- Prolongs life

Health Investment #2: Nutrition
- Water
- Plant foods

- Quality protein
- Healthy fats
- Supplementation

Hazardous Substances

- Sugar
- White flour
- Bad fat
- Artificial sweeteners

Health Investment #3: Sleep

- Try to establish and maintain a regular time for going to bed.
- Design a winding-down plan for the hour before bedtime.
- Turn off the television, and mellow out.
- Take some slow deep breaths as you relax in bed.
- Consider taking melatonin.
- Carb up (moderately) to increase your serotonin "feel good" hormone.

Health Investment #4: Recreation and Relaxation

- We need the balance of work and play.
- We need the contrast of rest and recreation.
- We need to take time to smell the roses.
- We need to have fun like children.

Investing for a Long, Healthy Life—
Maintaining Longer Telomeres

- Sleep seven to nine hours most nights.
- Take omega-3 supplements every day.
- Exercise six to seven days a week for maximum anti-aging benefits.
- Deal with your stress through healthy thinking and habits.
- Love life—attitude is almost everything.
- Take supplements to fill in your nutritional gaps.
- Eat at least thirty grams of fiber every day.
- Use olive oil instead of other vegetable oils.

- Drink green tea (or supplements).
- Never overeat.

WEALTH

Investing Principle #1: Consider Every Purchase as an Investment
- Programmable thermostat
- Warranties
- Mortgage refinance
- Energy Star appliances
- Health insurance

Investing Principle #2: Care for Long-Term
Savings: 401(k), TSP, SEP, or FIA
- Fund it.
- Forget borrowing from it!
- Feel free to roll over your fund.

Investing Principle #3: Maximize Short-Term Investments
- High-interest-bearing checking
- Nontraditional Certificates of Deposits
- Structured and laddered CDs

A Final Note on Investing
- Debt-free
- Savings full
- Retirement too

Chapter 9: De-Stress for Less

WEALTH

De-Stress for Less on the Run
- Things to do for free like going for walks, volunteering, and taking time for yourself

- Things to do inexpensively, such as movies at home, matinees, or discounted meals

De-Stress for Less When Going Out

- School discount cards
- Entertainment.com
- Facebook and Twitter
- Share and save
- Local newspaper
- Restaurant.com

De-Stress for Less on a Vacation

- Staycation
- Time-share freebies
- Share a time-share
- Two families for the price of one
- Home exchanges
- Volunteer-based vacations

HEALTH

The Overextended Life

- Stress kills, so take action to reduce it.
- Don't worry; be happy.
- Manage your "misery factor" with realistic expectations.

Energize Your Body to Minimize Your Stress

Stress Buster #1: Exercise

Stress Buster #2: Nutrition

Stress Buster #3: Sleep

Stress Buster #4: Have some fun!

Questions to Lighten Your Load

- Will this help me know and love my friends and family more?
- Will this help me grow in loving others more?
- Will this help me know and love God more?

Chapter 10: Raising Fit and Frugal Kids

WEALTH

Five Skills for Fiscal Success

Skill #1: The Allowance Lesson
- Budgets
- Discernment
- Saving
- Giving
- Values
- Delayed gratification

Skill #2: The Saving Lesson
- Long-Term savings account goals
- Family 401(k)
- Looney Tunes accounts
- Short-term goals
- Matching funds

Skill #3: The Sharing Lesson
- Give—Local church
- Gather—Groceries
- Give Again—Collect clothing and toys
- Gain—Sponsor a third-world child
- Give Some More—Bake for others

Skill #4: The Fun Budget Lesson
- Restaurant fun
- School supplies
- Amusement parks and zoos
- Clothing

Skill #5: A Strong Work Ethic Lesson
- Ensure your child's safety at a job.
- Make sure work is age appropriate.
- Provide on-the-job training.
- Be sure to follow through.
- Require quality work.

HEALTH

Growing Healthy Kids
- Be a strong role model.
- Use family-healthy self-talk.
- Motivate your children toward activity.
- Make changes slowly.
- Understand taste physiology.
- Provide creative "taste motivation" for young children.

The Top Five Nutritional Roadblocks for Young Children
Roadblock #1: Too much juice
Roadblock #2: Too many hydrogenated fats
Roadblock #3: Too much sugar and soda
Roadblock #4: Too little fiber
Roadblock #5: Too little protein early in the day

Chapter 11: Giving for Wealth and Health

WEALTH

Give to Charitable Organizations

- Local church
- Homeless shelters
- Crisis Pregnancy centers
- Women's shelters
- Food drives
- The Salvation Army, Goodwill Industries, and veterans

Give a Variety of Items

- Money
- Time
- Clothing
- Furniture
- Goods and Services

HEALTH

Give Generously

- The most generous gift of all is our time invested in others.
- Give the gift of healthy lifestyle modeling at home and with your friends.
- Give the gift of hope, health, and food to people in third-world countries.

Pay It Forward—Share Wealth and Health with Others Daily

- Share your health knowledge—without becoming a food/exercise tyrant.
- Share your food—invite someone to dinner.
- Share your hope.

Conclusion

A Few Words for the Walk

As you've learned within these pages and most likely in your own life, we all tend to follow the paths of least resistance. Fortunately, that is changeable if you give yourself some time and a little grace. We've discussed a variety of challenges and failure factors that tend to trip up many people. But remember, you never really fail unless you quit or give up. This is *your* life—don't give up on yourself!

It's not always the brilliant or exceptionally gifted people who succeed—sometimes it's the plodders who refuse to stop trying. If you simply show up and do something every day, you will make more progress than 80 percent of the population. Talk about the information you've found helpful in this book until the concepts come naturally. If you really want to master them, teach them to someone else.

Whatever you do, don't just put away this book, and go back to your old habits. Choose to be one of the 20 percent who moves from *knowing* to *doing*. Moving your knowledge to understanding—and your understanding to action—takes a little effort, but it is well worth it.

We wish you an incredible life of health and wealth!

—Ellie and Danna

Acknowledgments

We would like to thank our literary agent, Steve Laube, for the hard work he did in bringing this concept to fruition. He was the first to recognize that "Lean Body, Fat Wallet" was more than just a clever idea for a joint appearance with Danna and Ellie on ABC News. It was a big idea that could help others become healthier both physically and fiscally. Steve is a man of integrity and wisdom, and we are thankful for his guidance.

It has been a delight to partner with the entire team at Thomas Nelson who have enthusiastically embraced our project. From Brian Hampton, who saw the potential of marrying two unique lifestyle areas into one practical book, to the entire editorial and marketing team—our entire experience has been pure joy. Kristen, Chad, Katherine, Emily, and Kimberly: Your support, energy, and fresh ideas have encouraged us all along the way. You are the dream team most authors can only wish to have—and you have all exceeded our highest expectations. All we have left so say is, "Wow!"

Notes

CHAPTER 1: HABITS FOR HEALTH AND WEALTH

1. *Merriam-Webster's Dictionary*, s.v., "habit" (Springfield, MA, 2008), www.merriam-webster.com/dictionary/habit.
2. To author in a conversation with Gail Hayes, quote calling herself "an igniter of purpose." Used with permission.

CHAPTER 2: THE YOU ARE WHAT YOU THINK HABIT

1. Caroline Leaf, PhD, *Who Switched Off My Brain?* (Nashville: Thomas Nelson, 2009), 82.
2. Ibid., 83.
3. Shadhelmstetter (YouTube user), "Dr. Shad Helmstetter—'The Story of Self-Talk,'" April 30, 2008, http://www.youtube.com/watch?v=rvzfnm9uk-0.
4. Archibald Hart, *Habits of the Mind* (Dallas: Word, 1996), 158.
5. *Lean Bodies . . . Fat Wallets Self-Talk* CD can be ordered at www.leanbody-fatwallet.net.
6. Shawn Achor, *The Happiness Advantage* (New York: Crown Publishing Group, 2010).

CHAPTER 3: THE 3D HABIT

1. Stephen R. Covey, *The 7 Habits of Highly Effective People* (New York: Simon & Schuster, 1989).
2. The Money, Meaning, and Choices (MMC) Institute, "Mission of the Money, Meaning, & Choices Institute," accessed July 10, 2013, http://www.mmcinstitute.com/about-2/mission.
3. George Bernard Shaw, *Man and Superman* (CreateSpace Independent Publishing Platform, 2004).

4. Shaun King, "Do It Alone, Person to Person," *Huffington Post*, February 22, 2012, http://www.huffingtonpost.com/shaun-king/do-it-alone-person-to-per_b_1293231.html.

CHAPTER 4: THE IN AND OUT HABIT
1. International Food Information Council (IFIC), 2012 Food and Health Survey, www.foodinsight.com/foodandhealth2012.aspx.
2. Frank M. Sachs et al., "Comparison of Weight-Loss Diets with Different Compositions of Fat, Protein, and Carbohydrates," *New England Journal of Medicine*, 360, no. 9 (February 26, 2009), 849–852.

CHAPTER 5: THE SUSTAINABLE LIFESTYLE HABIT
1. Jeff Olson, *The Slight Edge* (Lake Dallas, TX: Success Books, 2005, 2011), 15.
2. Stephen R. Covey, *The 7 Habits of Highly Effective People* (New York: Simon & Schuster, 1989), 151.

CHAPTER 6: BALANCED BODIES AND BUDGETS
1. Jane Kirby, RD, *Dieting for Dummies*, 2nd ed. (Hoboken, NJ: John Wiley & Sons, 2003), 59.

CHAPTER 7: FAT CELLS AND FAT SALES
1. Roy Baumeister and John Tierney, *Willpower* (London: Penguin Books, 2012), 80.
2. Roy Baumeister et al., "Ego Depletion: Is the Active Self a Limited Resource?" *Journal of Personality & Social Psychology*, 74, no. 5 (1998): 1252–1265.
3. USDA, "Cost of Food at Home," modified June 26, 2013, http://www.cnpp.usda.gov/usdafoodcost-home.htm.
4. Shawn Achor, *The Happiness Advantage* (New York: Crown, 2010), 162.

CHAPTER 8: HEALTHY INVESTMENTS FOR BODY AND BANK
1. Michael Fossel, Greta Blackburn, and Dave Woynarowski, *The Immortality Edge: Realize the Secrets of Your Telomeres for a Longer, Healthier Life* (Hoboken, NJ: John Wiley and Sons, Inc., 2011).
2. Ibid., vii.

CHAPTER 9: DE-STRESS FOR LESS

1. Claire Barthelemy, "Poll: Money Worries World's Greatest Cause of Stress," CNN.com, September 30, 2009, http://www.cnn.com/2009/WORLD/americas/09/30/stress.survey.money.
2. Lawrence Chilnick, *Heart Disease: An Essential Guide for the Newly Diagnosed* (Philadelphia, PA: Perseus Books Group, 2008).
3. "How Does Stress Affect Us?" American Psychological Association, accessed July 10, 2013, http://psychcentral.com/lib/2007/how-does-stress-affect-us.
4. Gene Wallenstein, *Mind, Stress, and Emotion: The New Science of Mood* (Boston, MA: Commonwealth Press, 2003).
5. Bruce McEwen, *The End of Stress as We Know It* (Washington, DC: Joseph Henry Press, 2003).
6. "How Does Stress Affect Us?" American Psychological Association.
7. Quoted in *When All You've Ever Wanted Isn't Enough: The Search for a Life that Matters* by Harold Kushner (New York: Kushner Enterprises, 1986), 161.

CHAPTER 10: RAISING FIT AND FRUGAL KIDS

1. Quoted in *What Every Child Needs* by Elisa Morgan and Carol Kuy Kendall (Grand Rapids: Zondervan, 1997), 122.
2. Joseph M. Mercola, D.O., "Aspertame: Safety Approved in 90 Nations, but Damages the Brain," September 26, 2012, http://articles.mercola.com/sites/articles/archive/2012/09/26/aspartame-causes-brain-damage.aspx.

CHAPTER 11: GIVING FOR HEALTH AND WEALTH

1. To sponsor a child, please visit: www.worldvision.org.

About the Authors

Ellie Kay is the best-selling author of fifteen books including *The 60 Minute Money Workout* and *Living Rich for Less*. She is a popular international speaker, and as a media veteran and spokesperson, she has appeared on more than eight hundred radio/TV stations, including CNBC, CNN, and Fox News. Ellie is married to Bob, a retired USAF fighter pilot. The Kays have a gaggle of seven financially savvy and physically fit young adult children.

Danna Demetre describes herself as a "work in progress" who loves to inspire others toward living more intentional lives. A former registered nurse, marketing manager for a Fortune 500 financial company, and fitness professional, she has combined her years of varied experience and become a well-respected lifestyle expert. Danna is a popular retreat and conference speaker and author of several books. However, she considers her roles as wife and mother the most important. She lives in San Diego with her husband, Lew, and their seventeen-year-old adopted grandson, Jesse. They also have three married adult children and four other grandchildren. You can learn more about Danna at www.DannaDemetre.com.